COLORING CBOOK AND MEMORY GAME

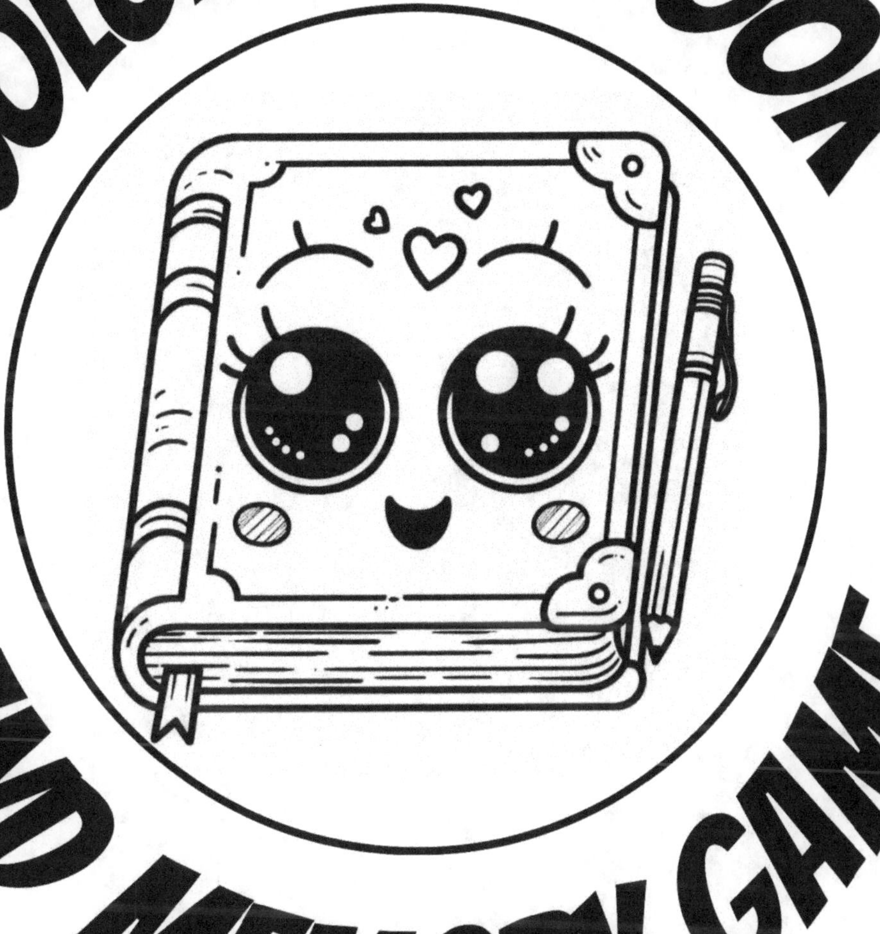

I am grateful to God for everything! And I believe that the meaning of life is to give meaning to other lives. May we extend this gratitude to everyone around us.

Silvaneth Santos

2024

THIS BOOK BELONGS TO

AGE 3 TO 12

All Rights Reserved

No part of this publication may be reproduced, or transmitted in any form or by any means, including photocopying, recording, or other electronic or mechanical methods, without the prior written permission of the publisher, except for brief quotations incorporated in critical uses. Any unauthorized reproduction of this work is prohibited.

2024

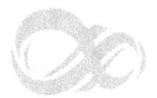

HELLO THERE!

This book offers a fun and educational experience, combining a coloring book with a memory game. Readers can bring a variety of animals to life while exercising their creativity, and also challenge their concentration and observation skills with the memory game. A unique opportunity to learn in an engaging and interactive way.

Ready? Let's Start.

TEST COLOR PAGE

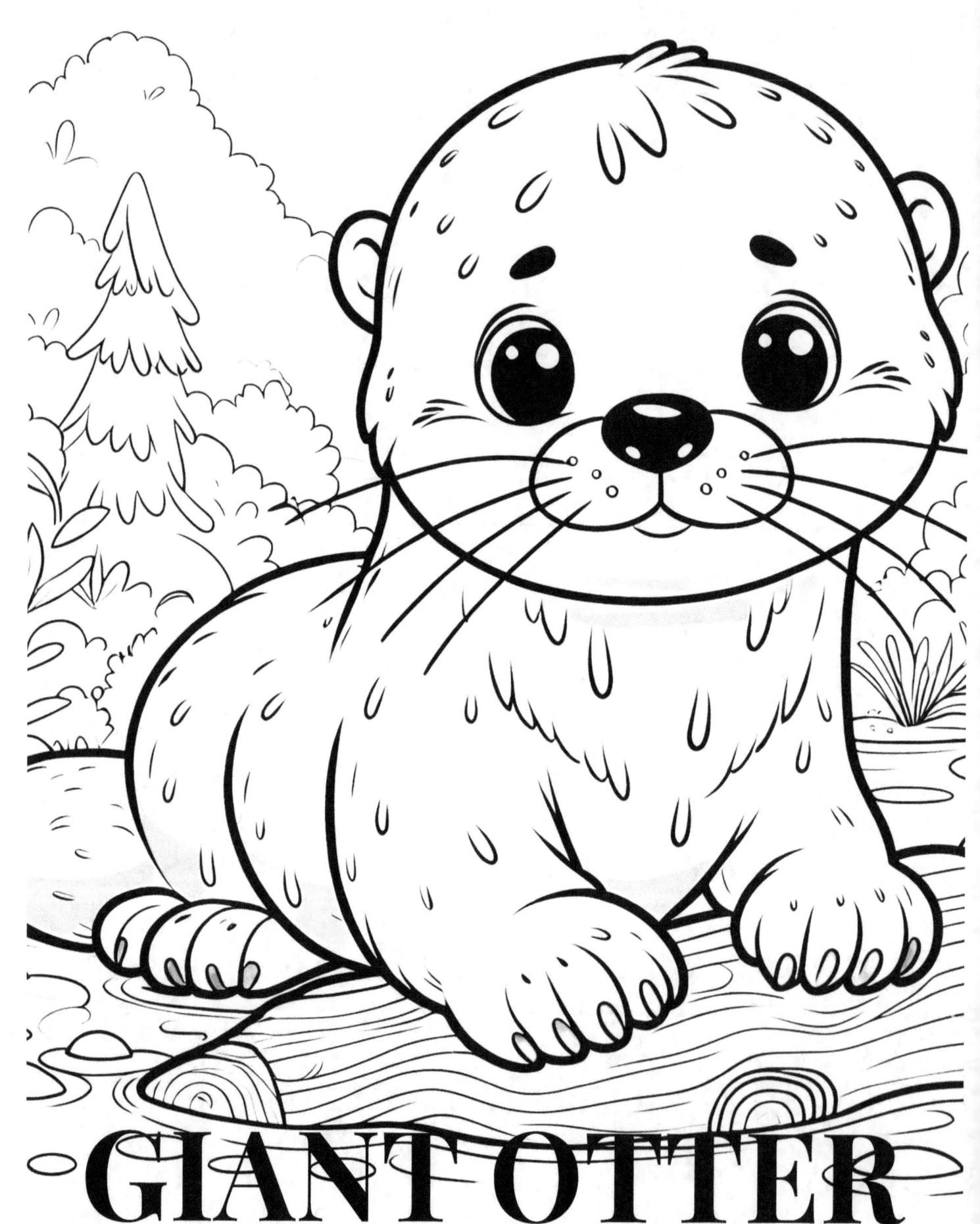

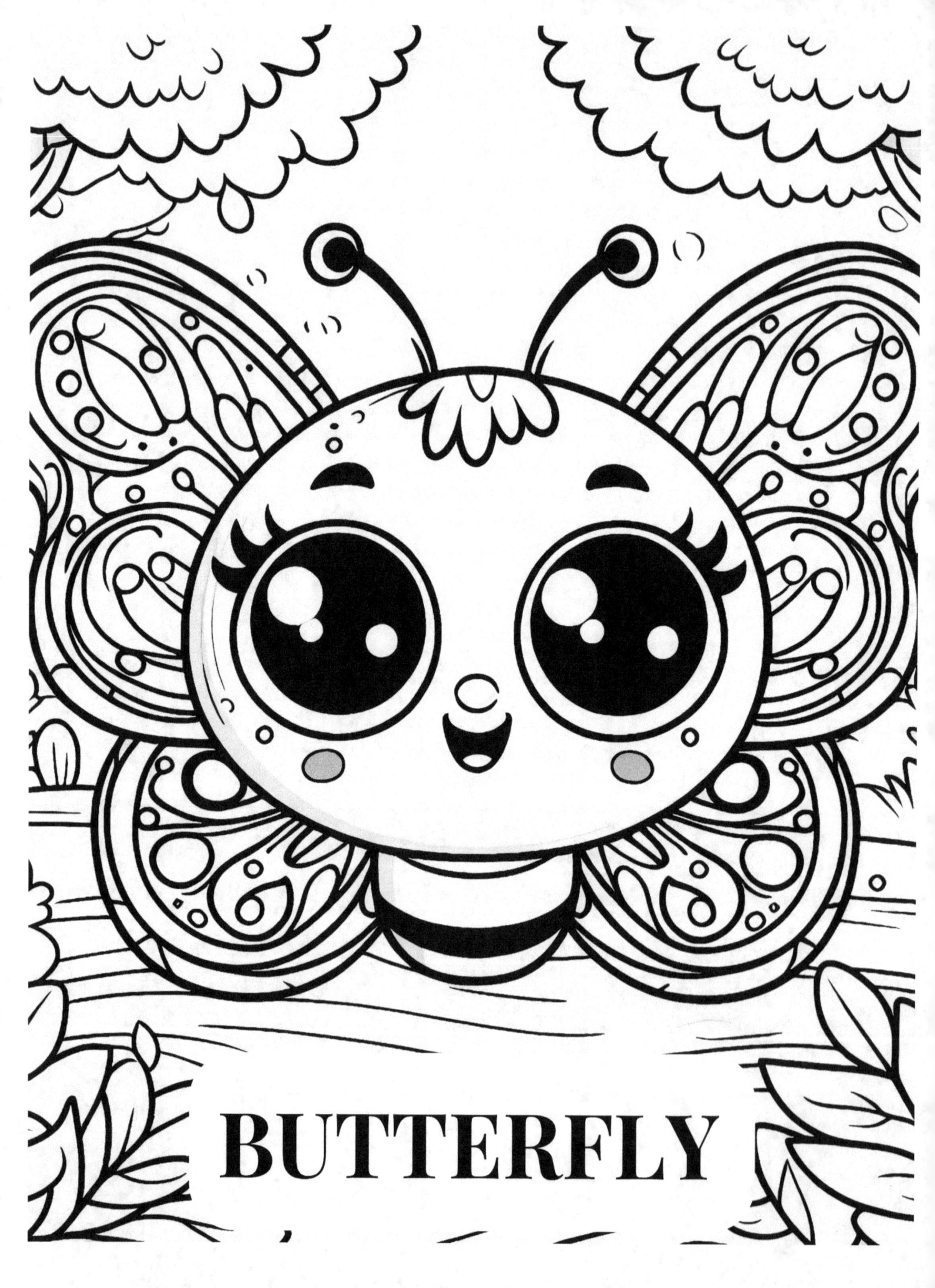

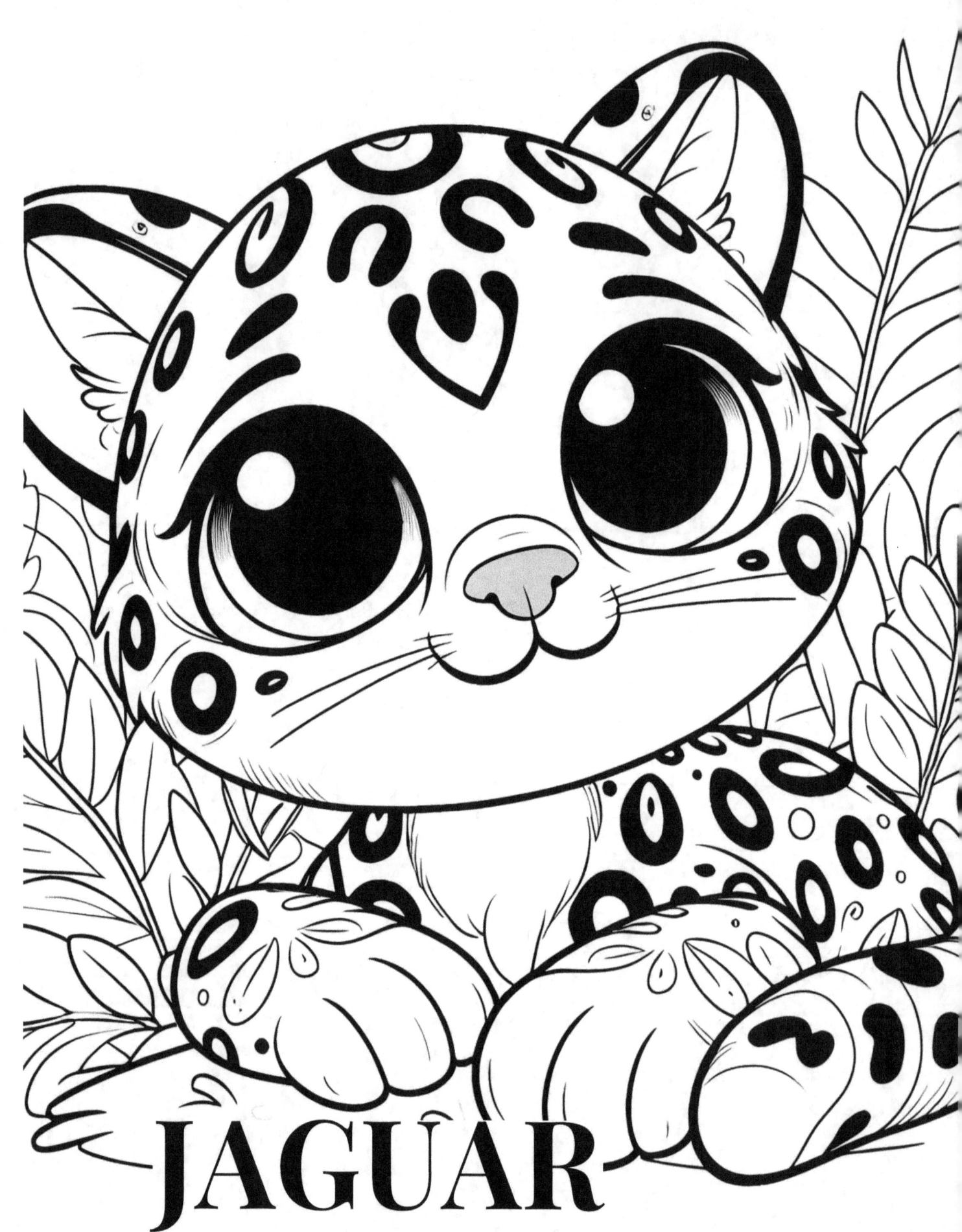

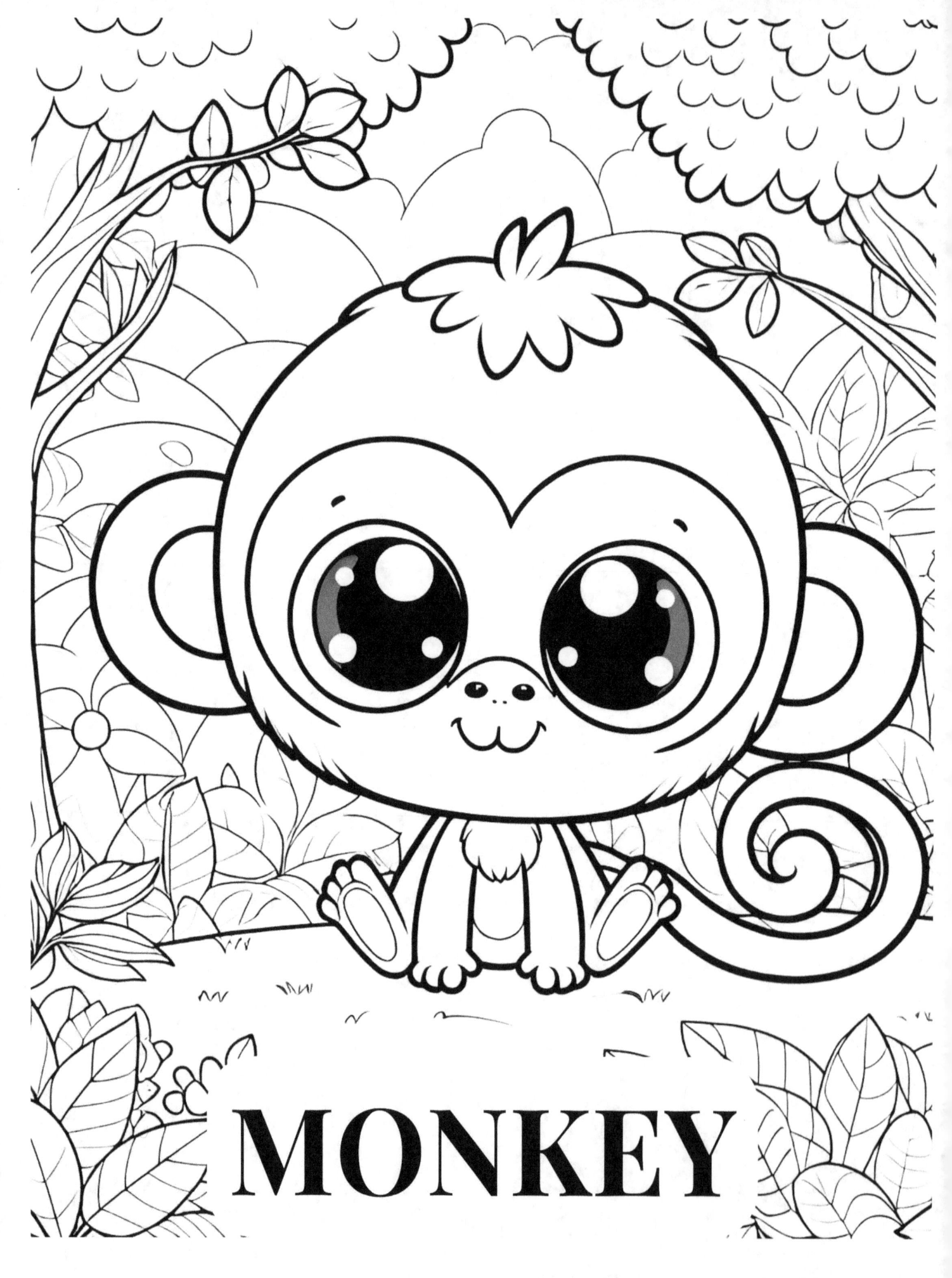

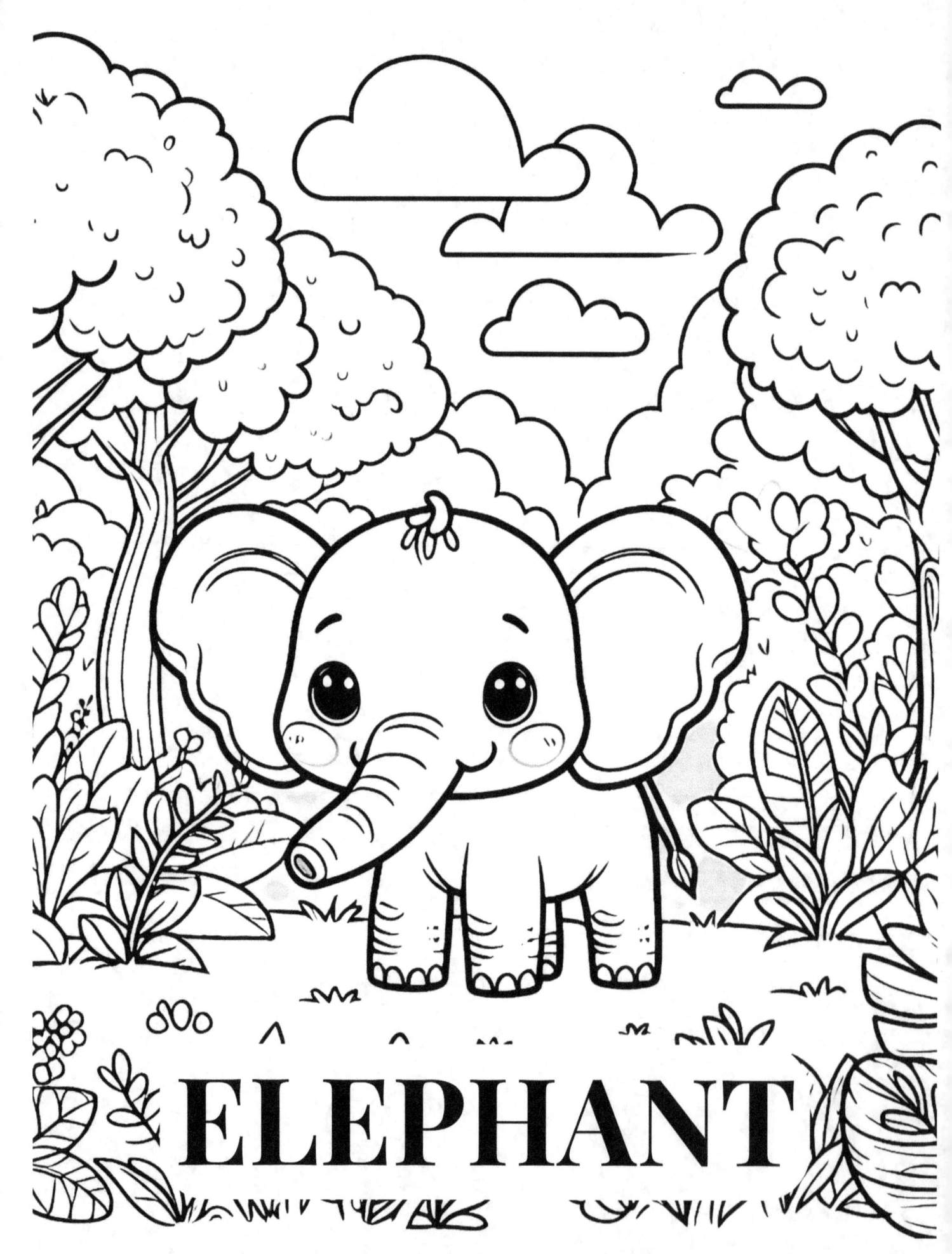

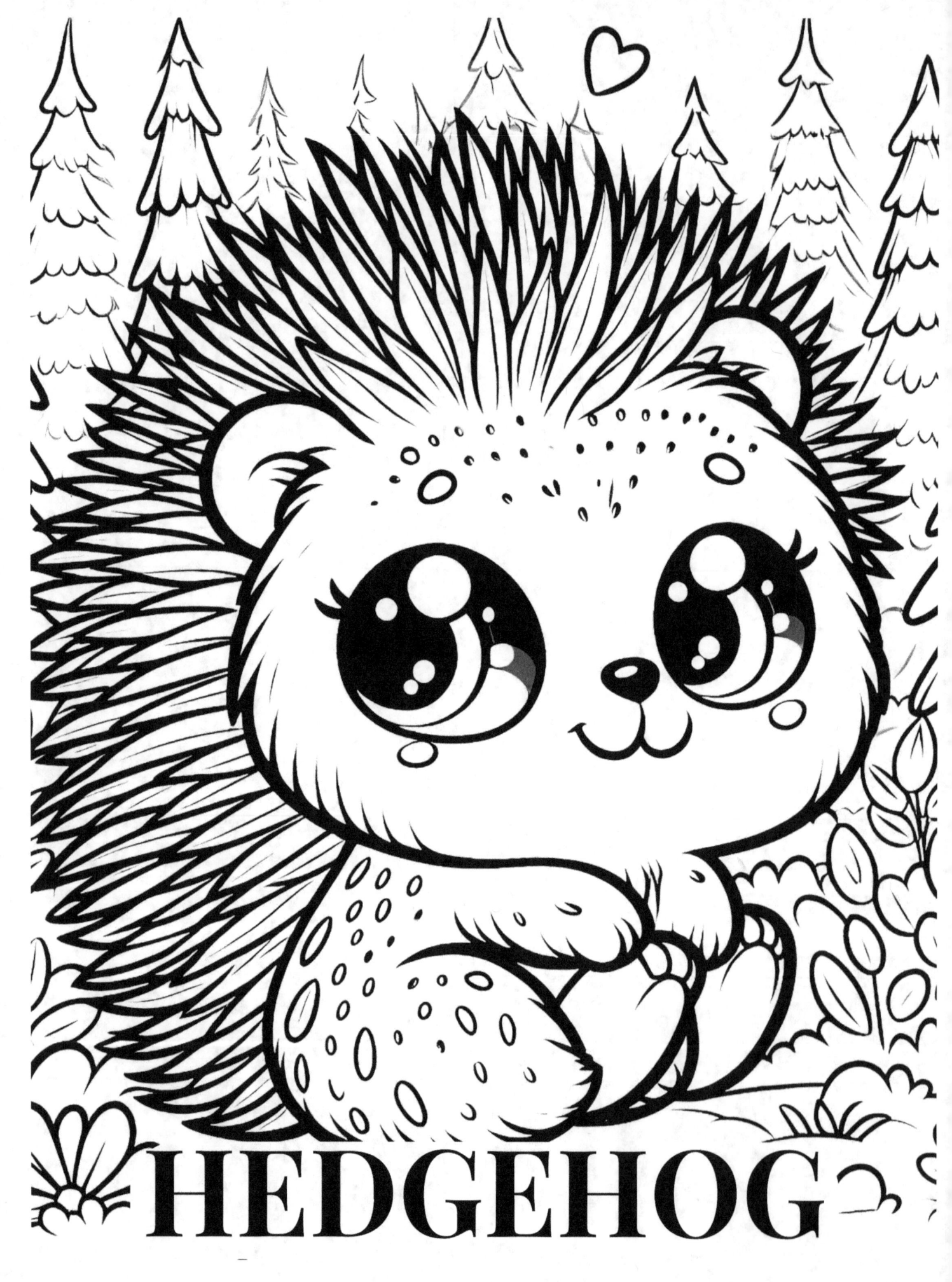

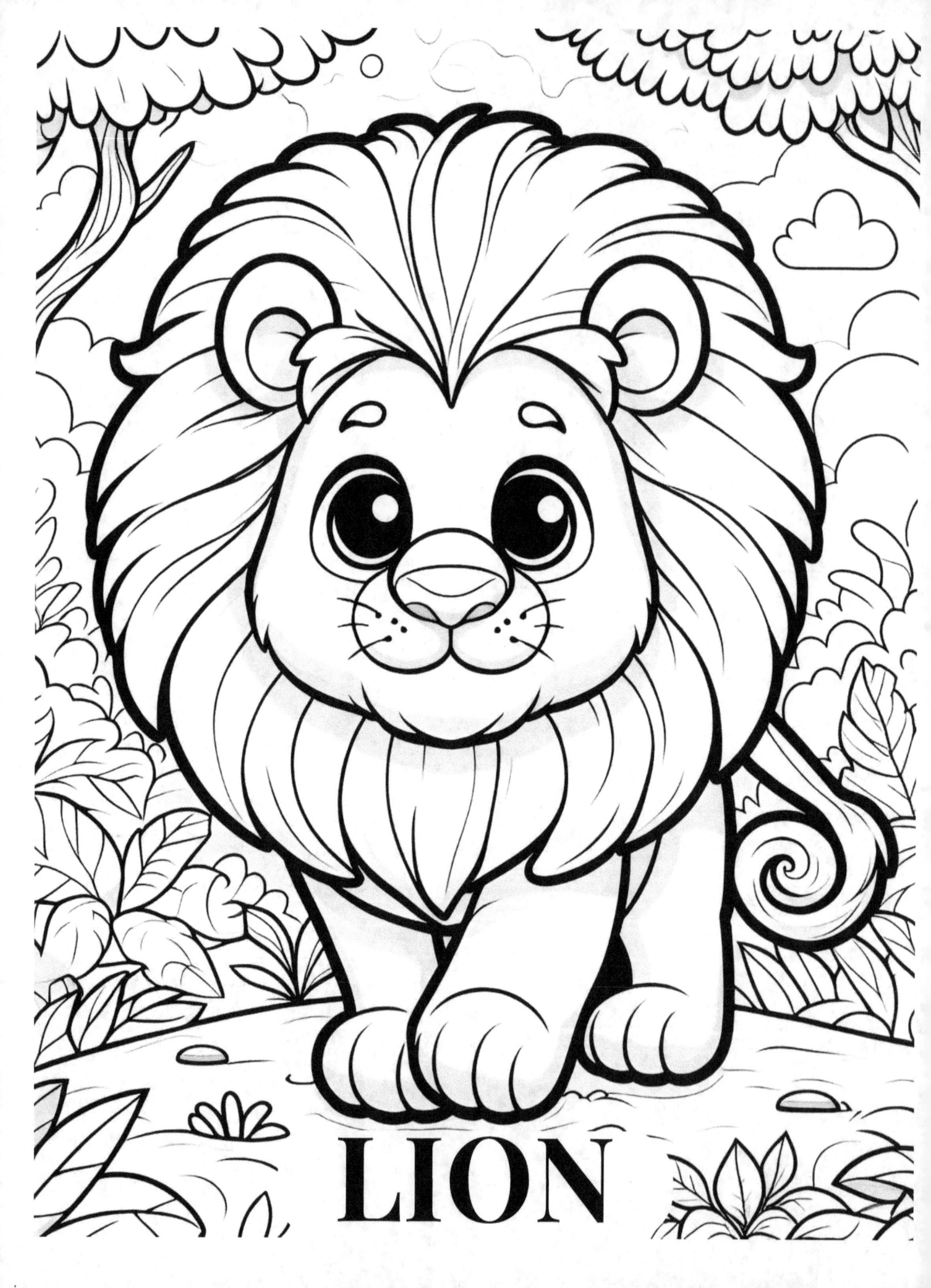

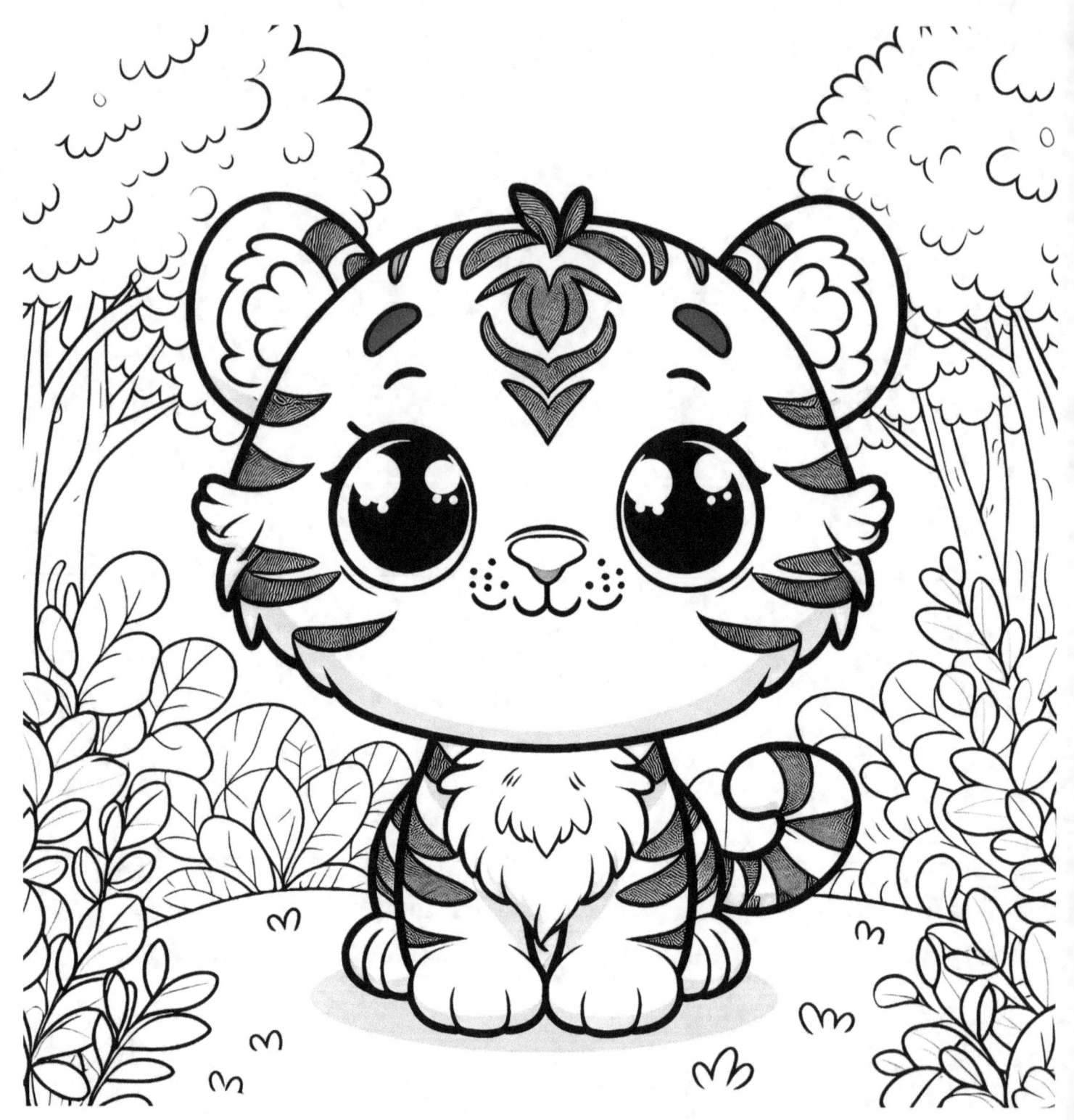

TIGER

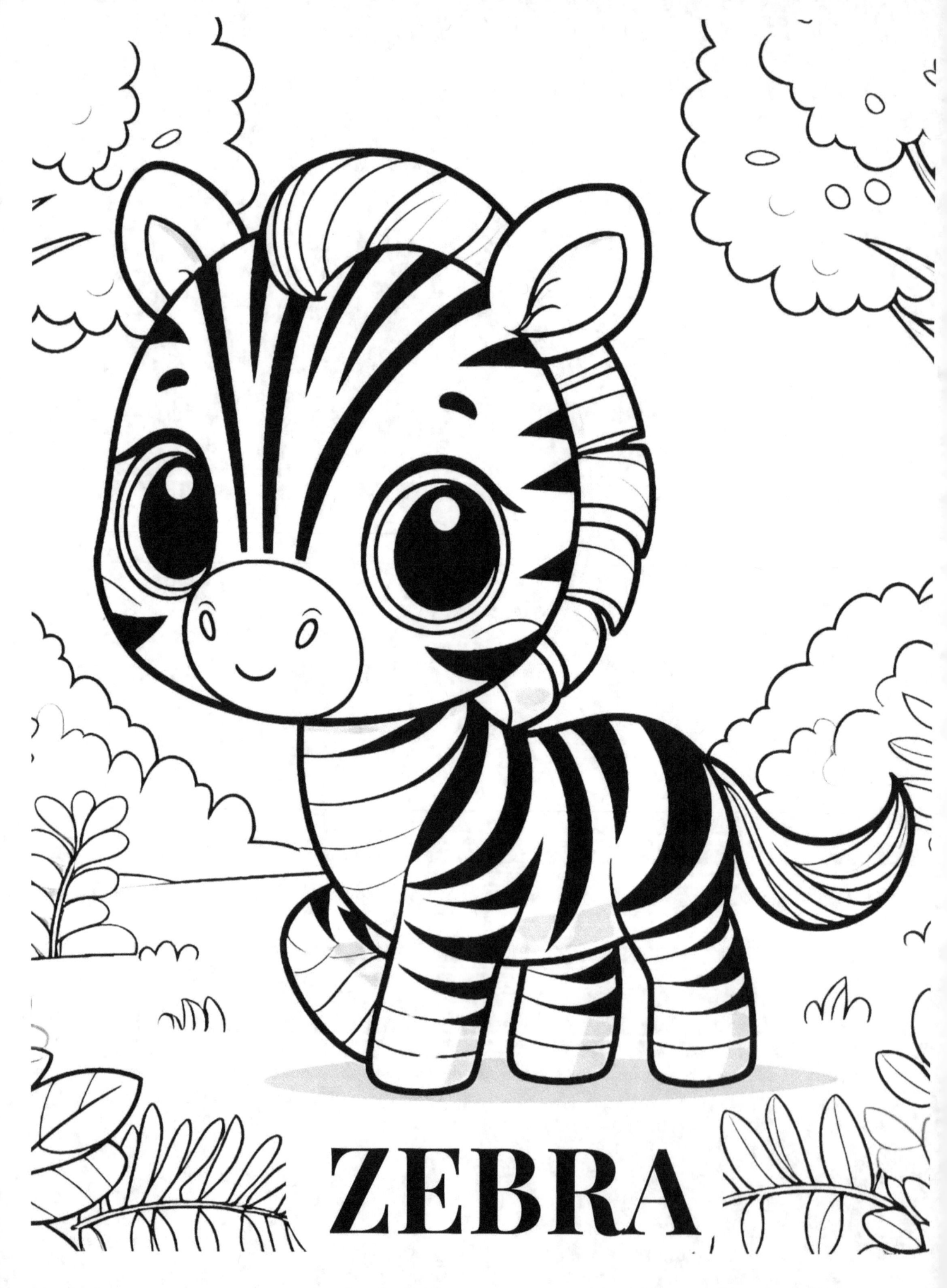

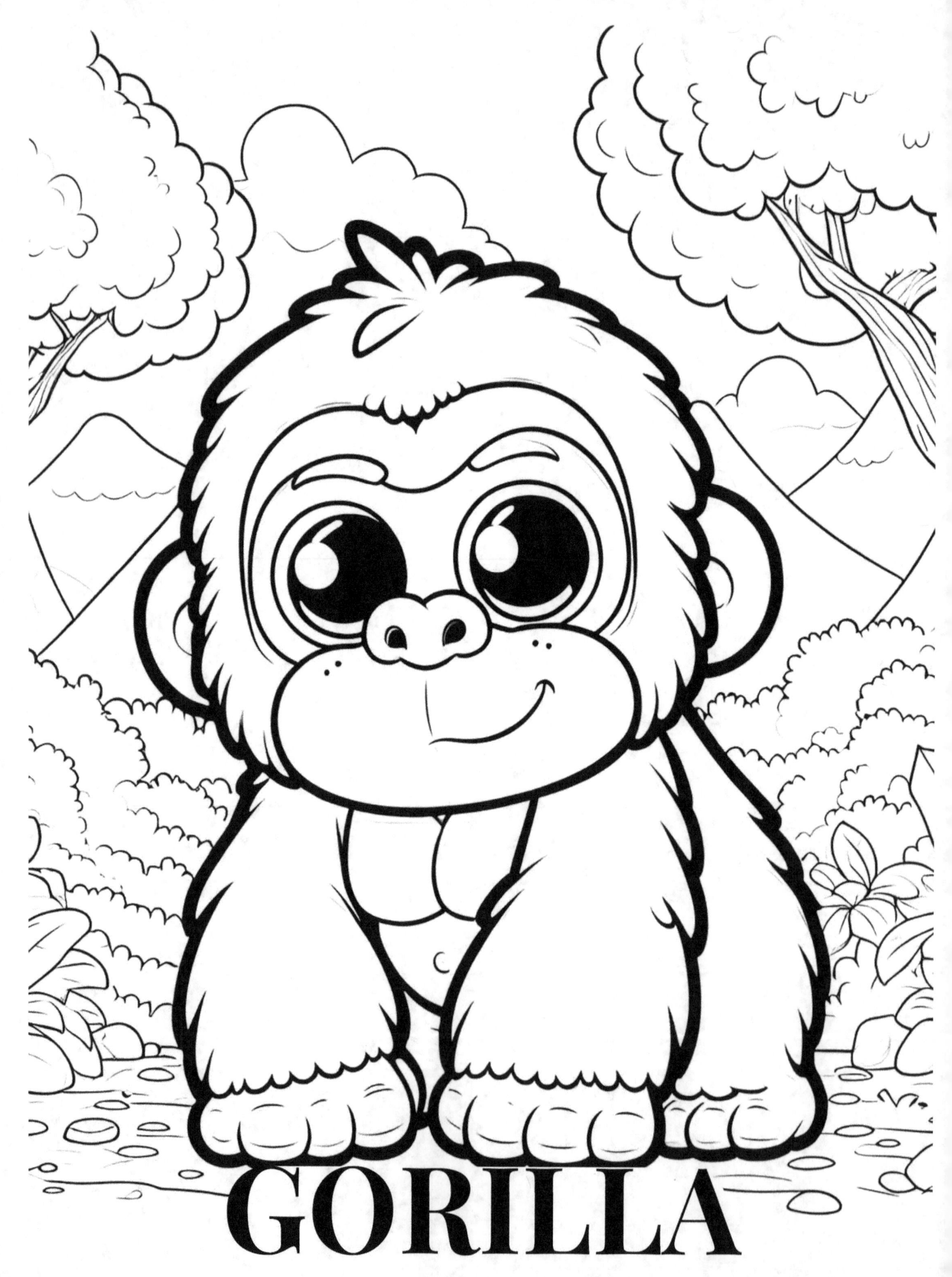

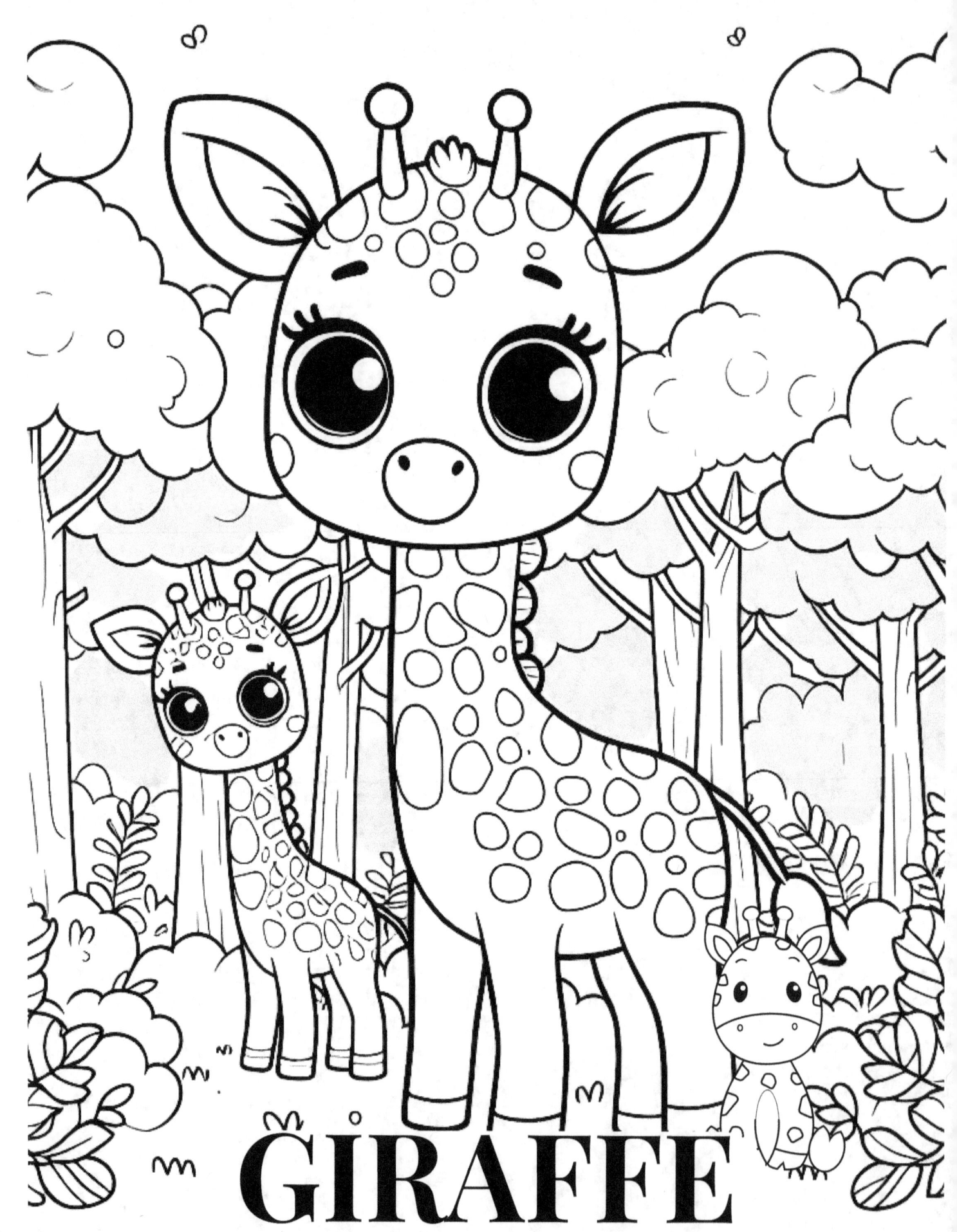

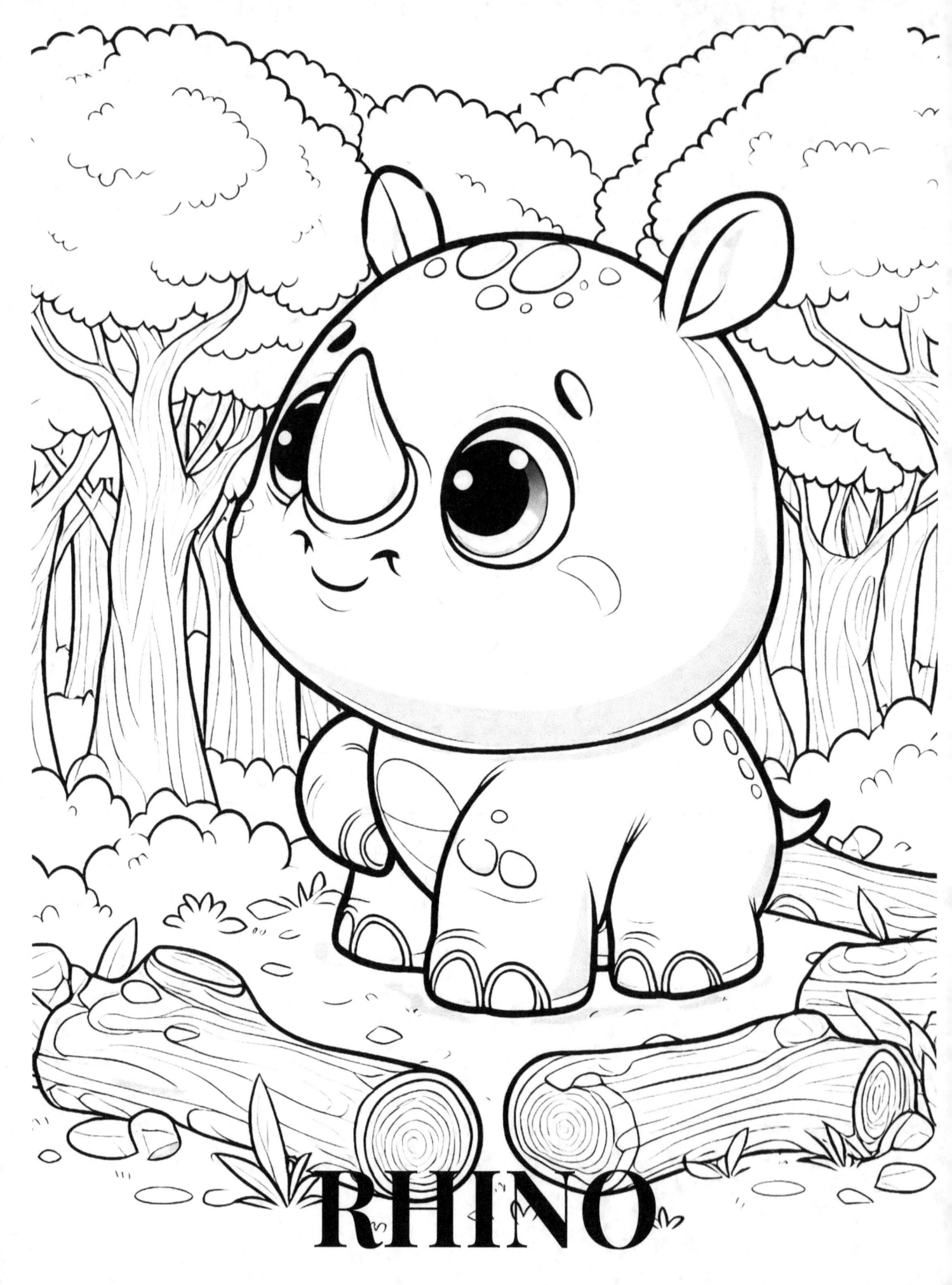

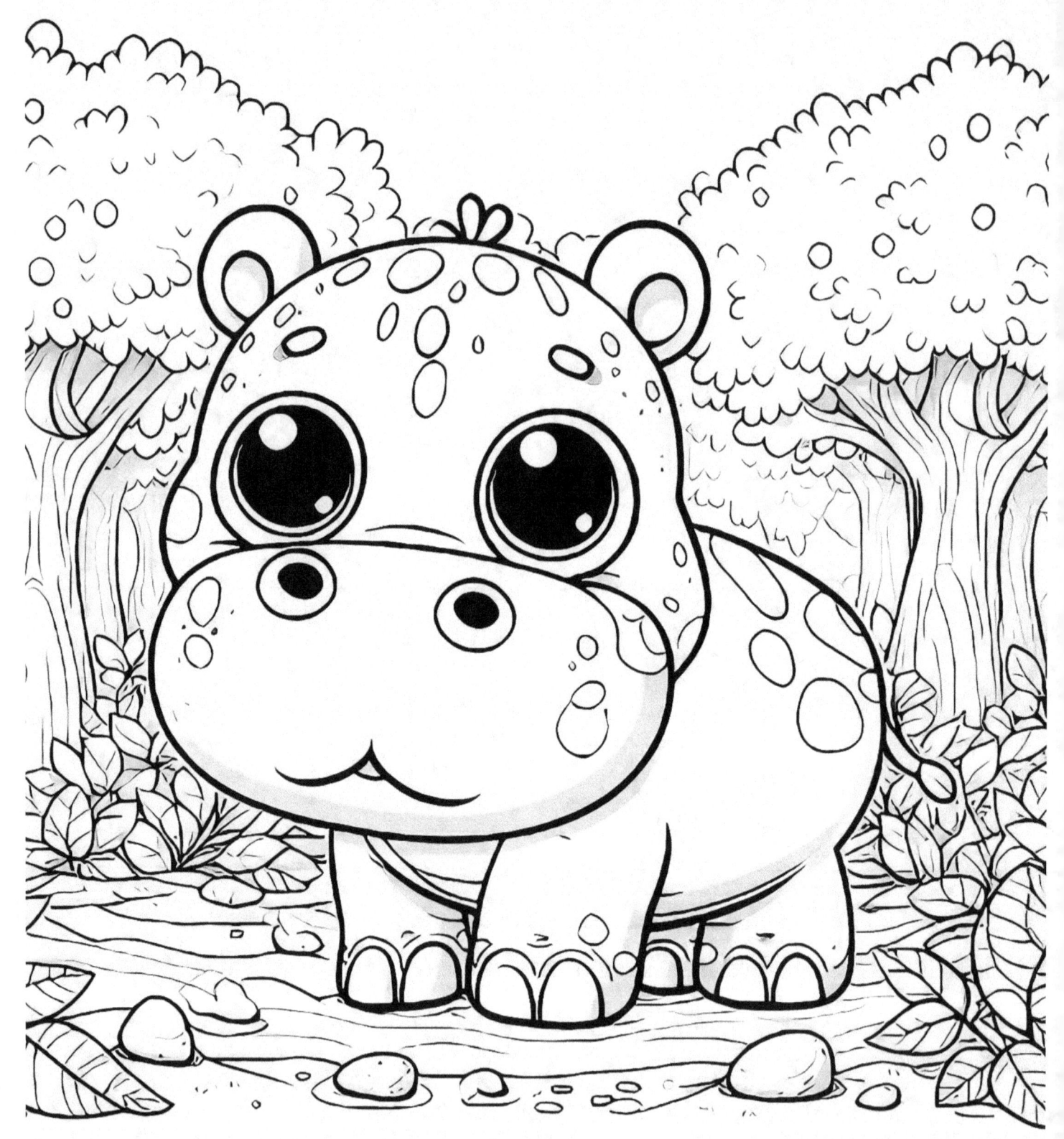

HIPOPPOTAMUS

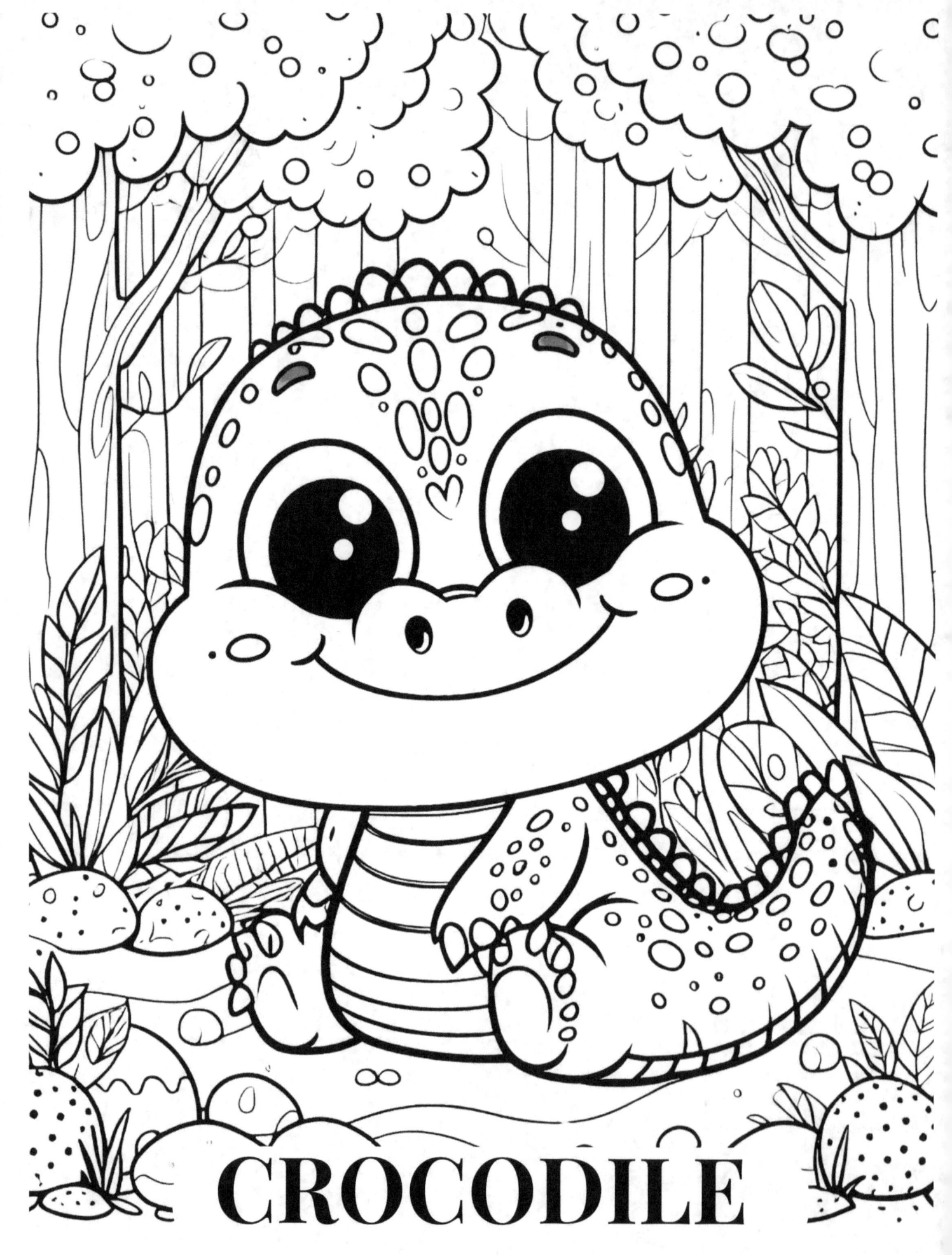

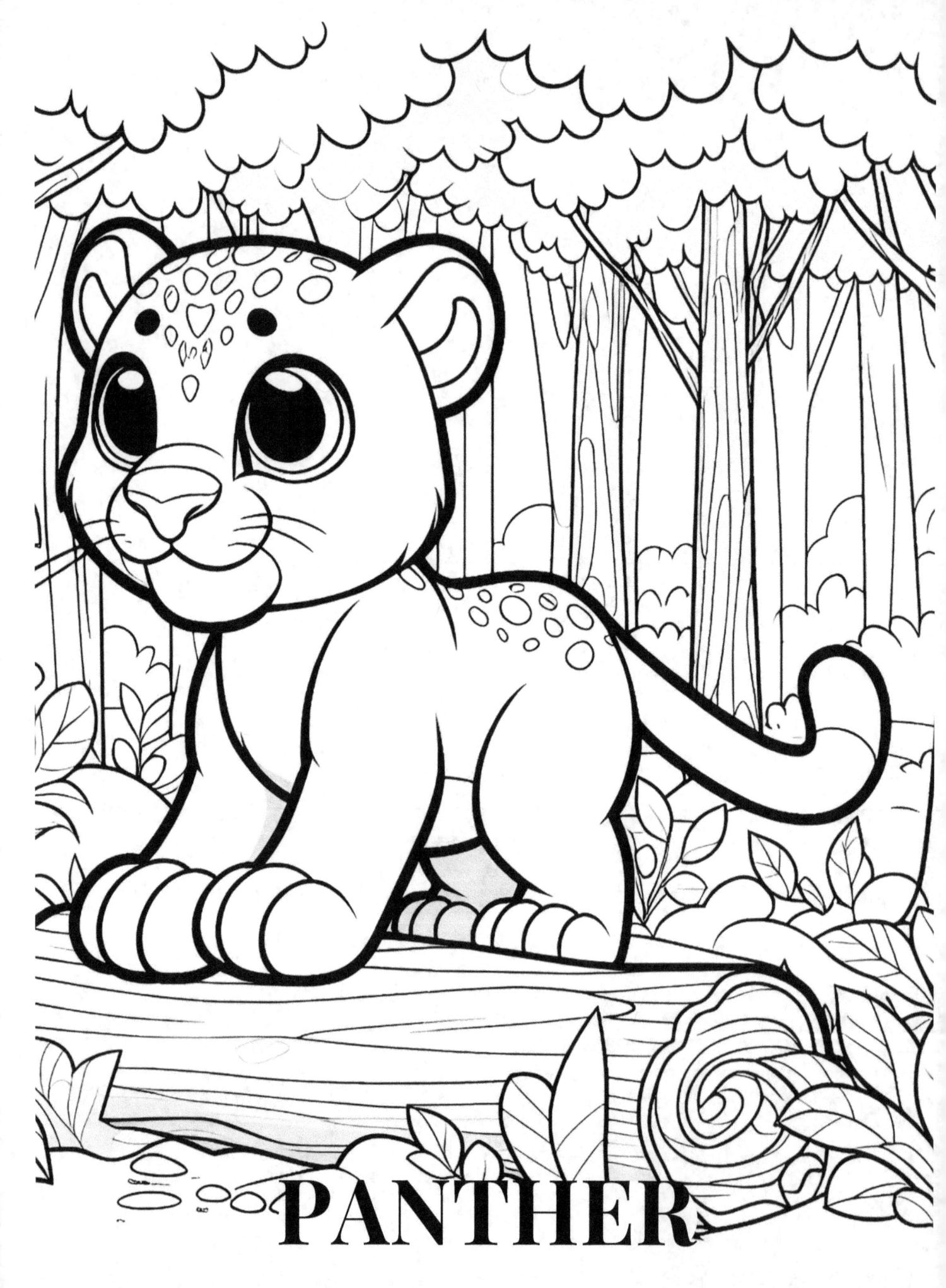

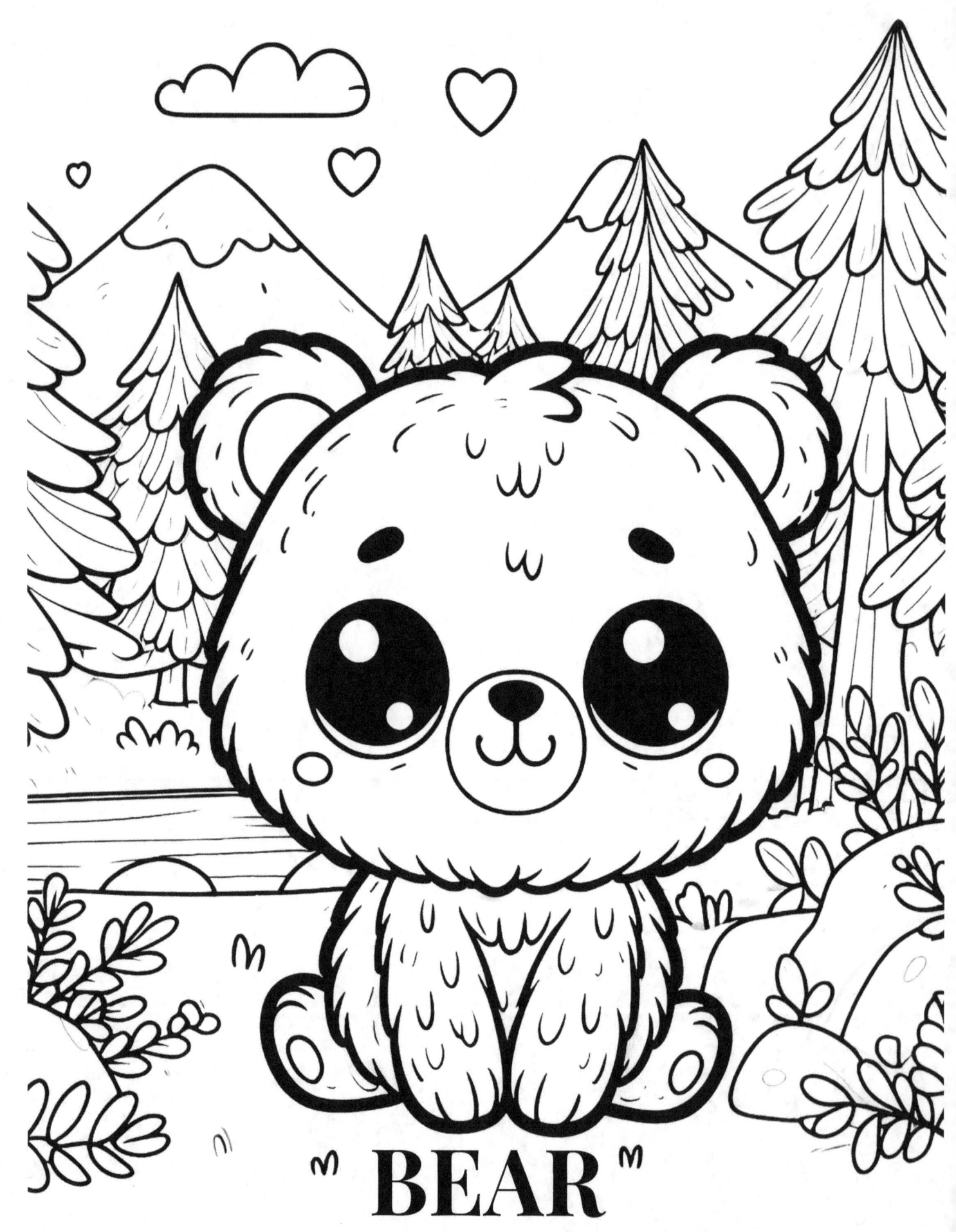

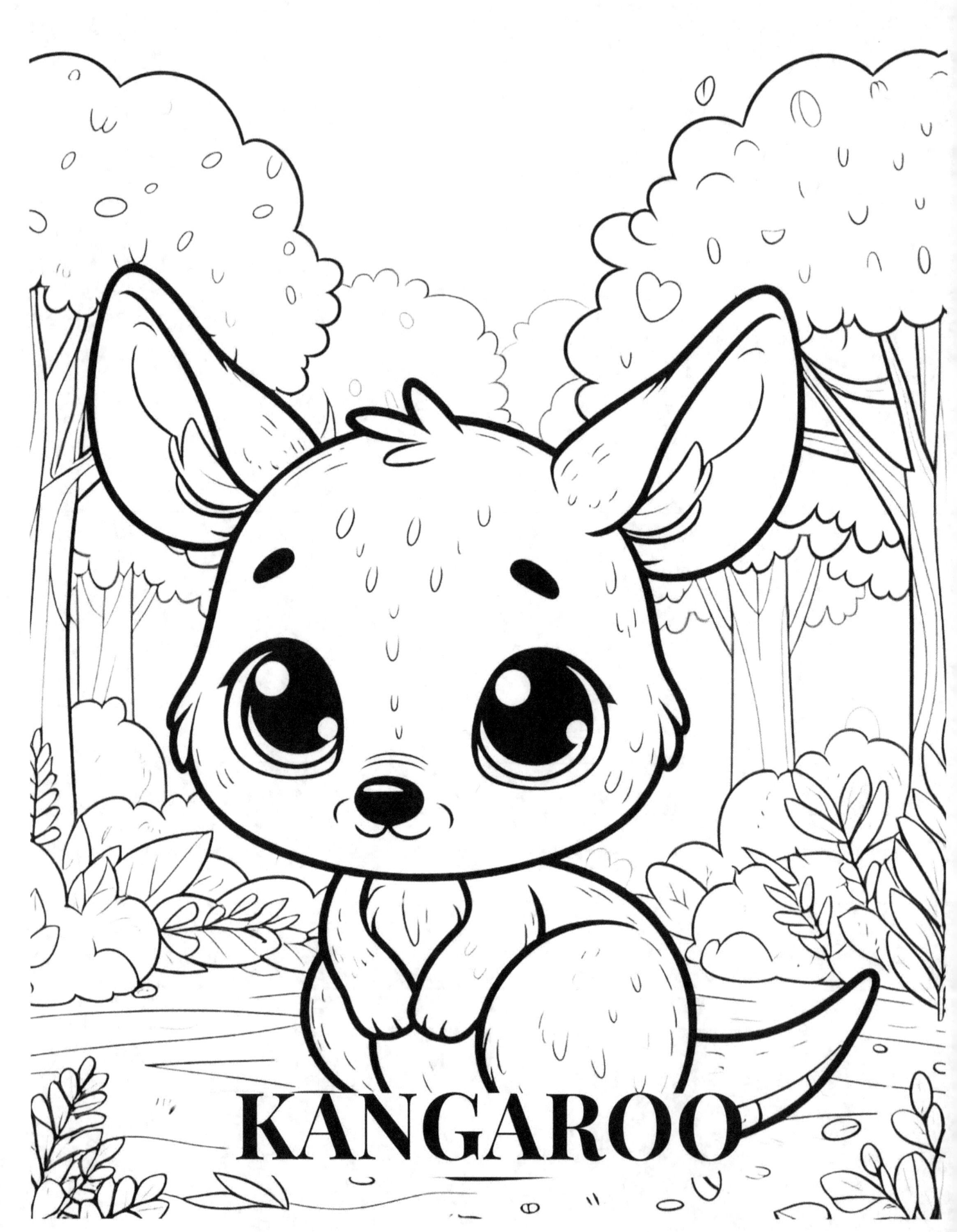

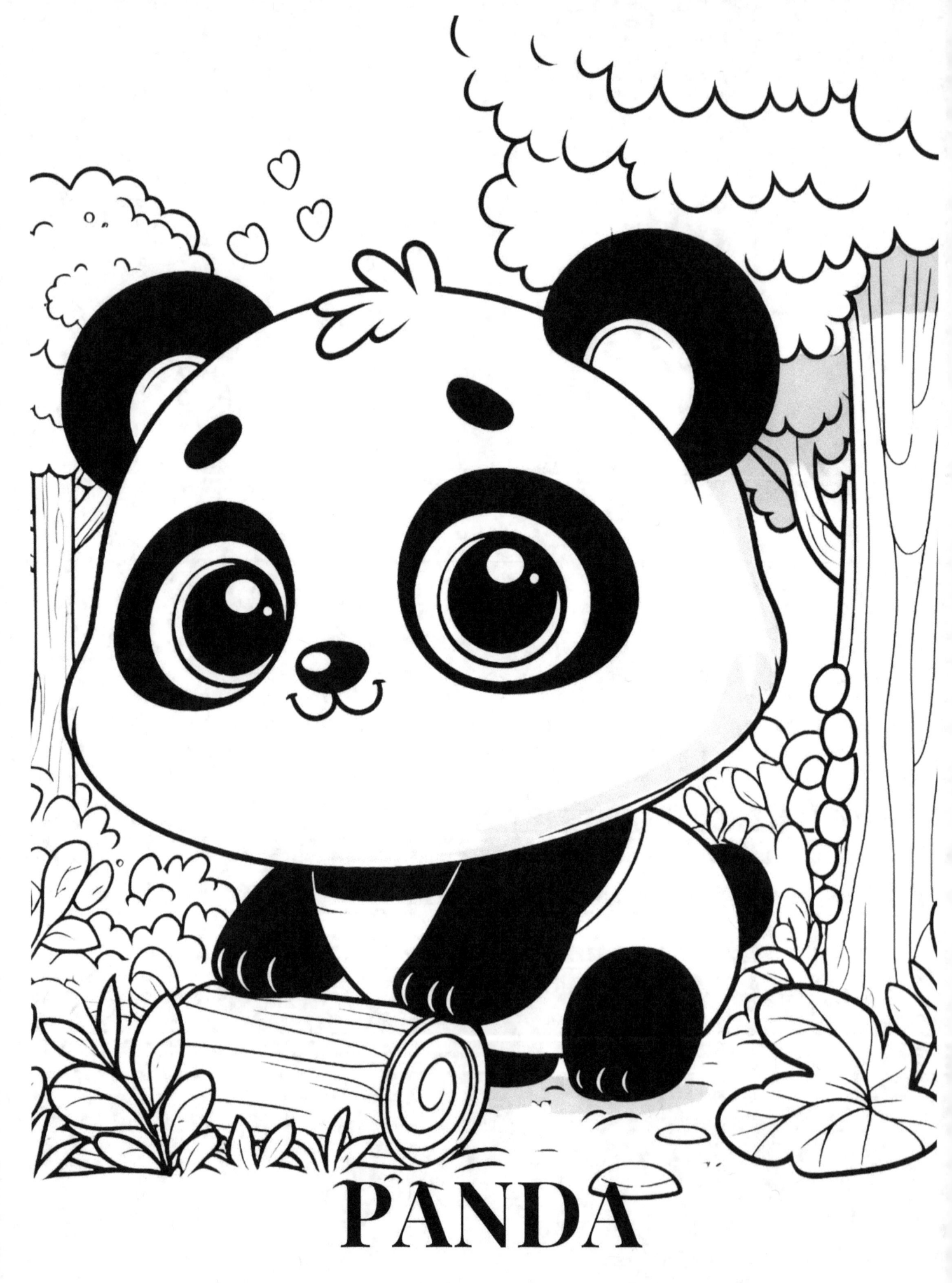

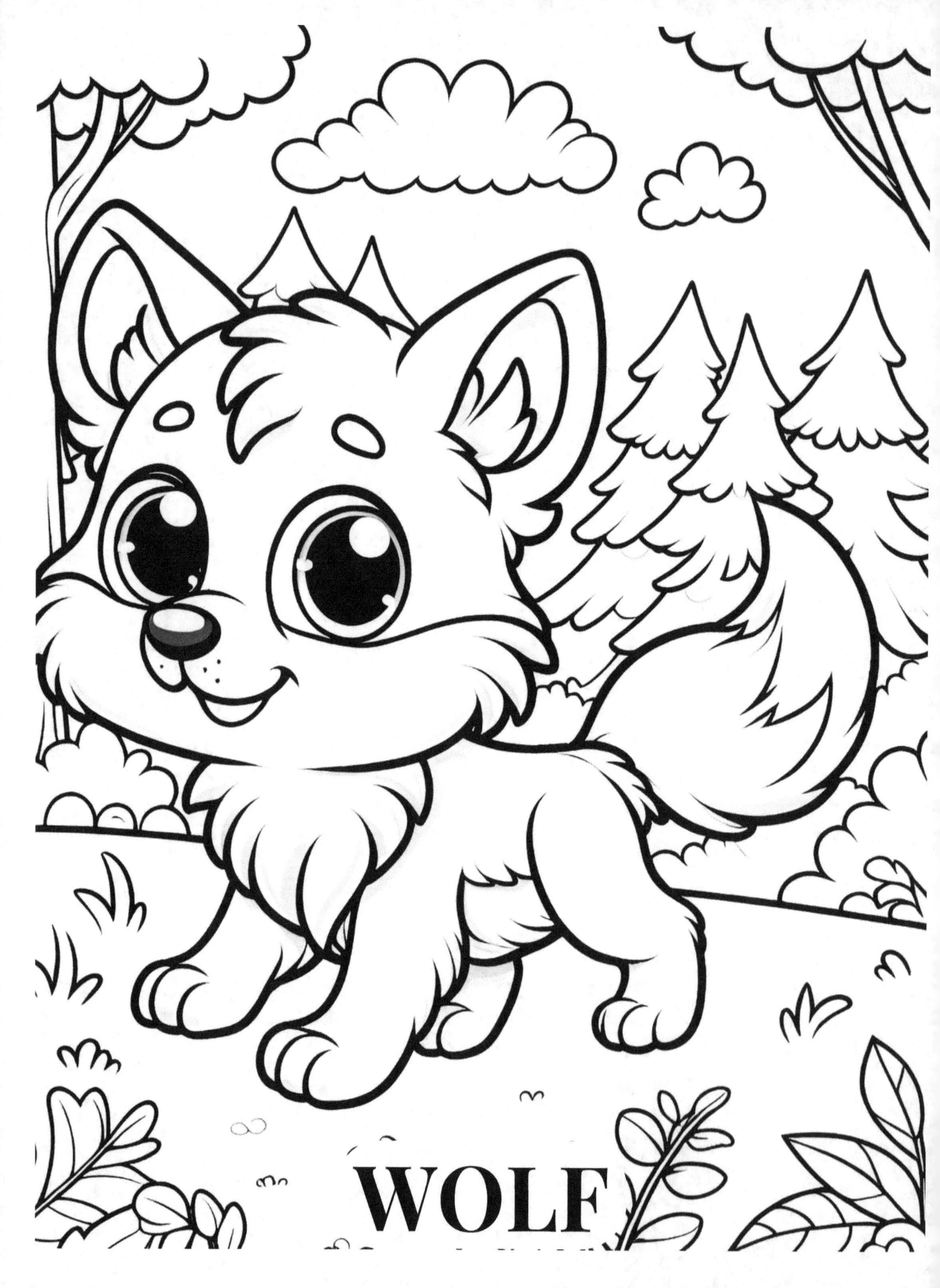

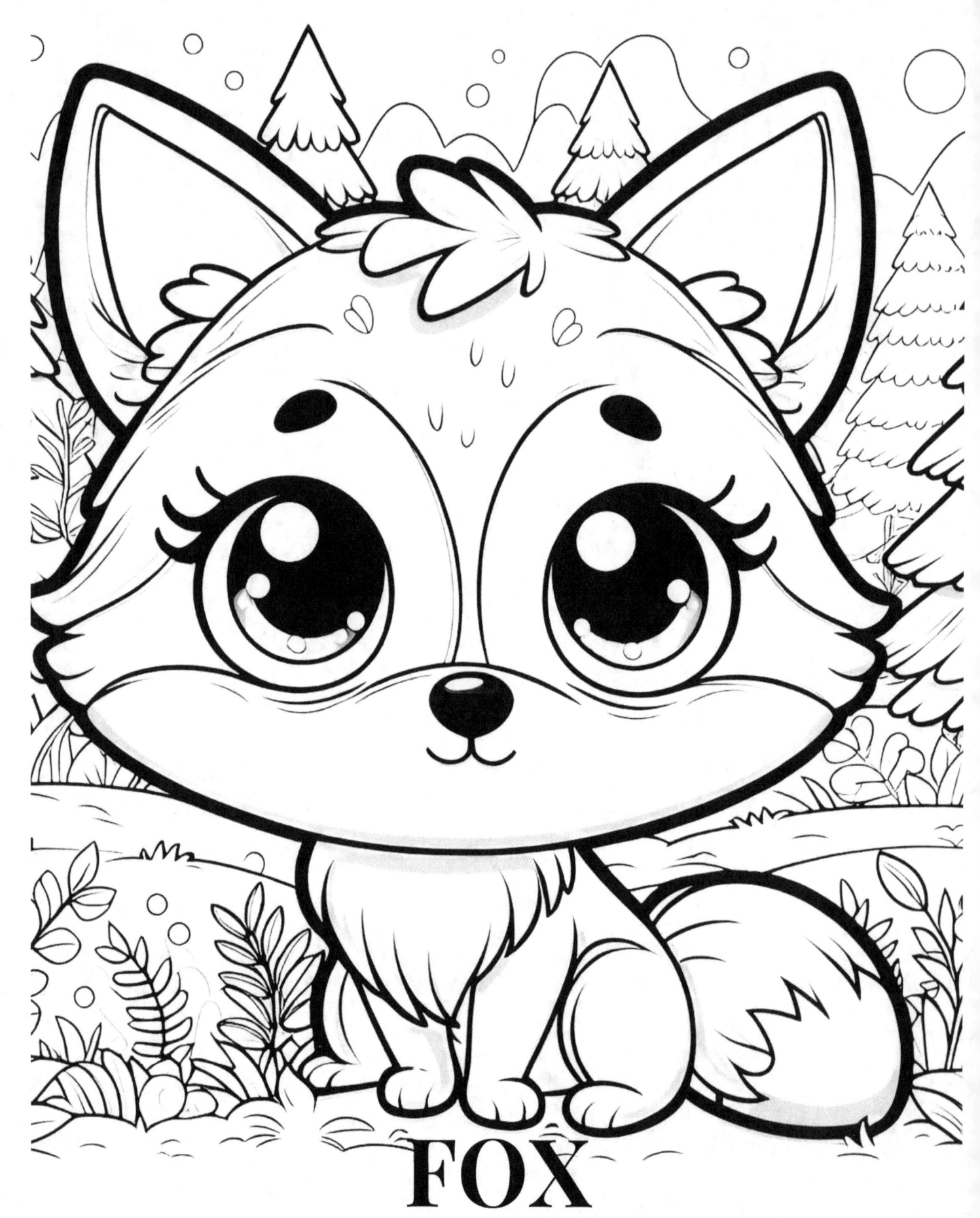

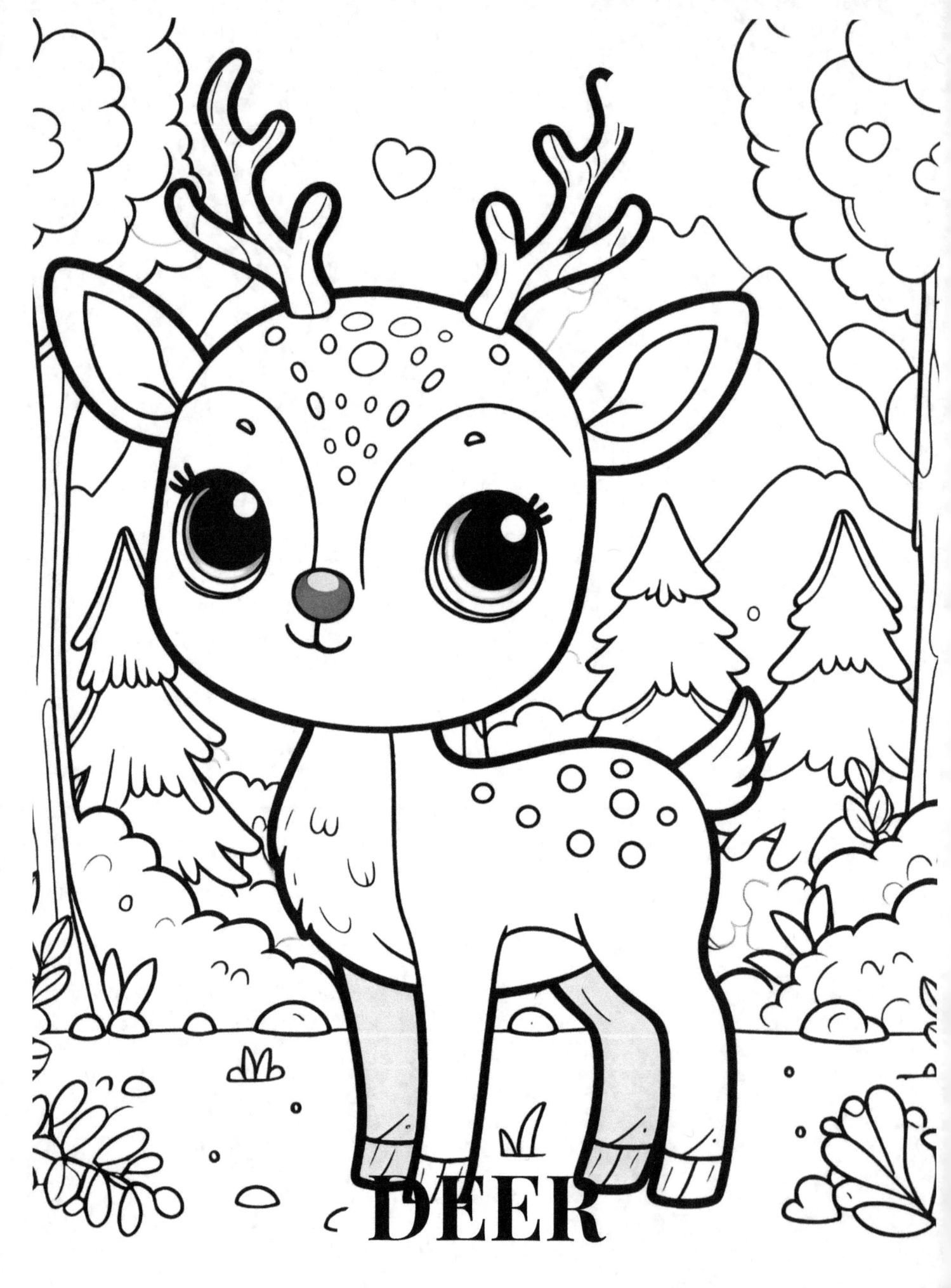

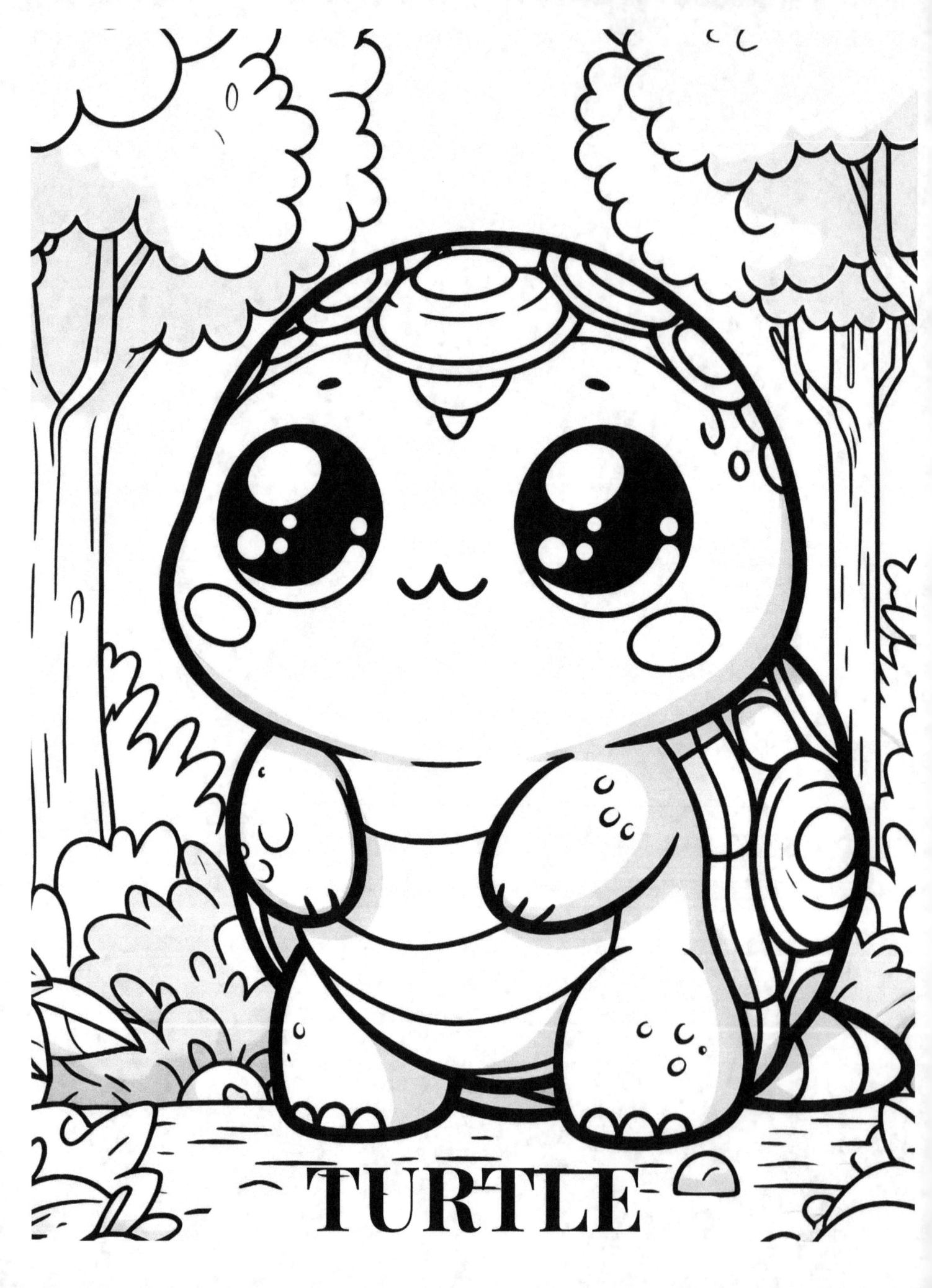

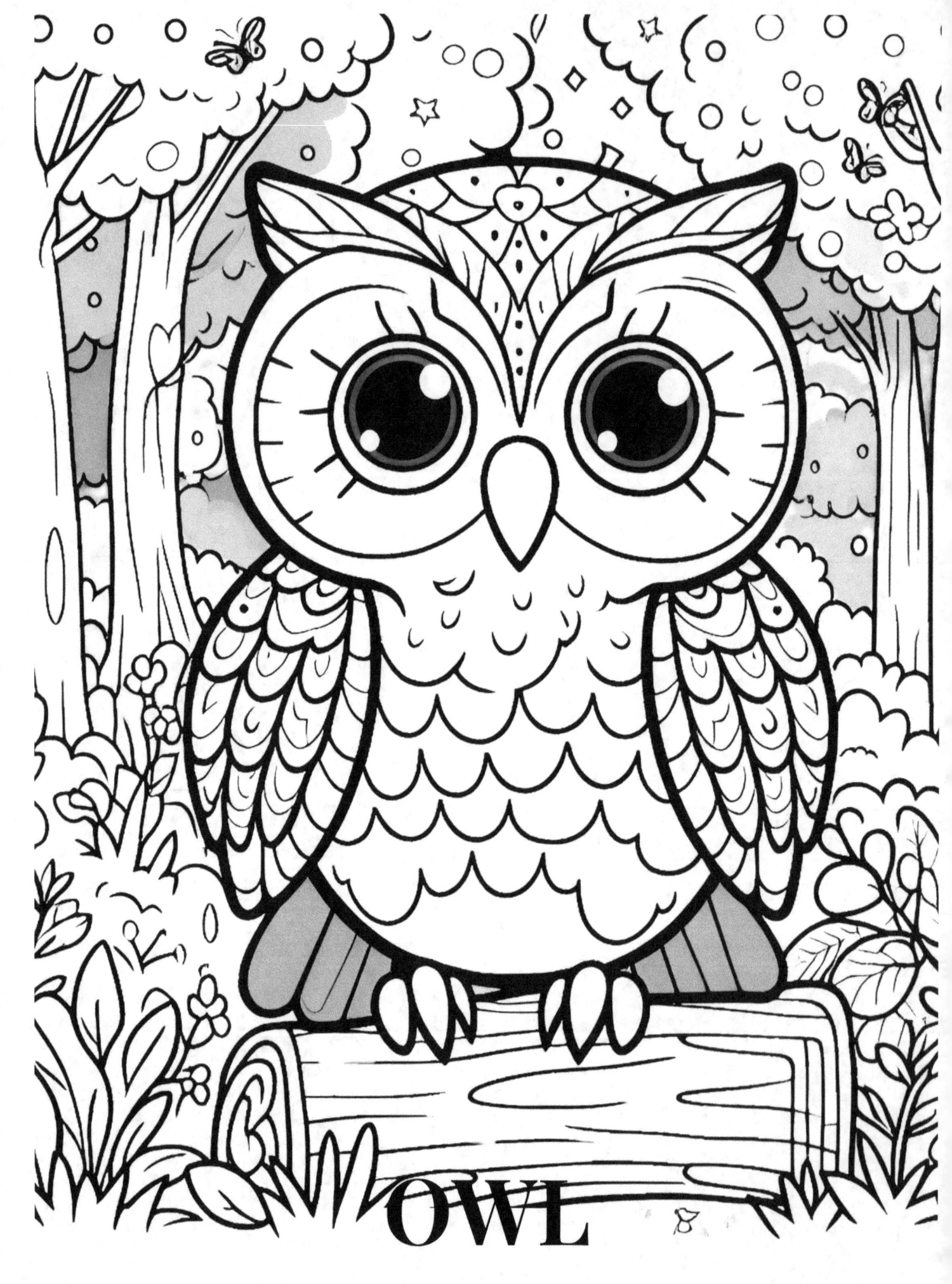

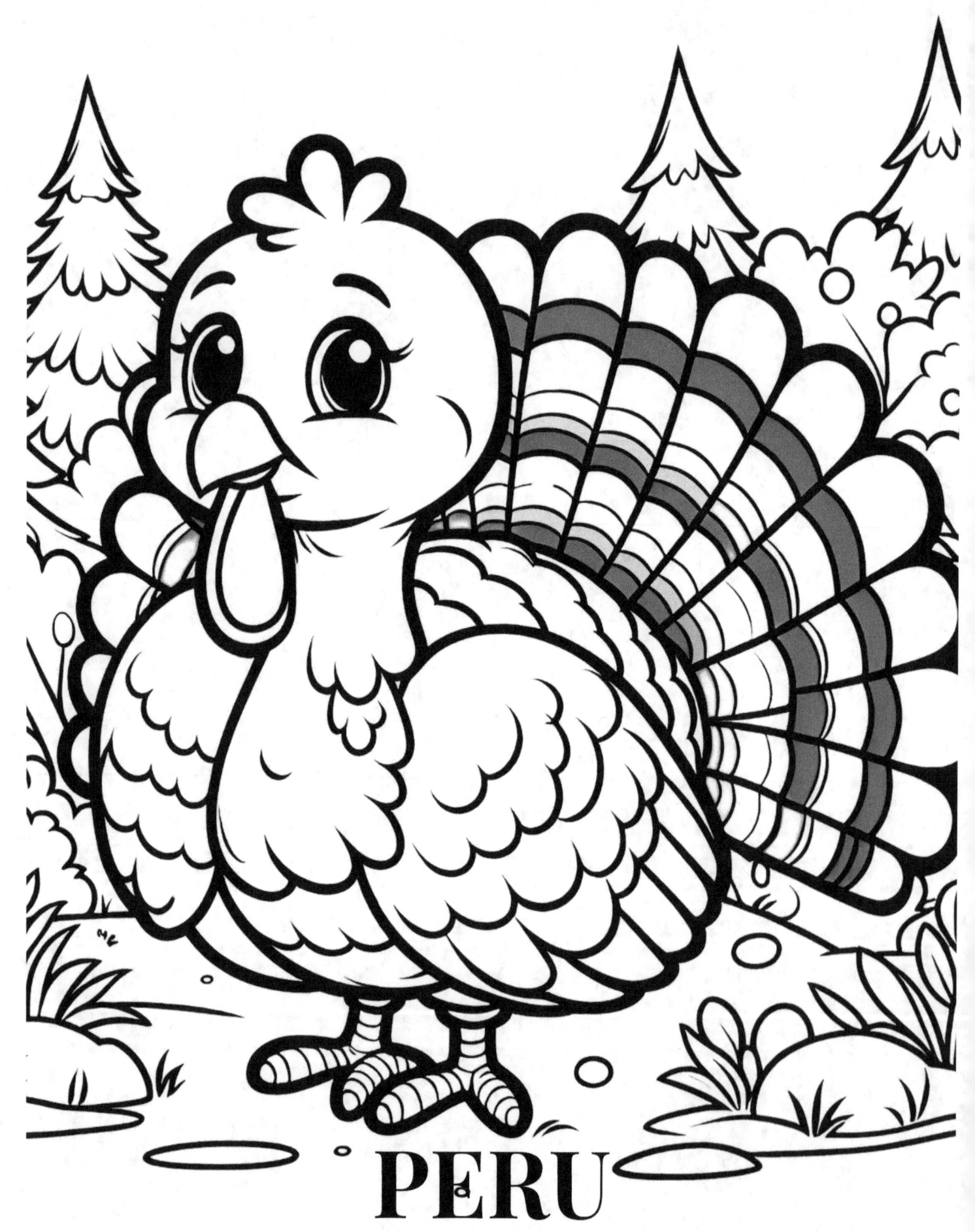

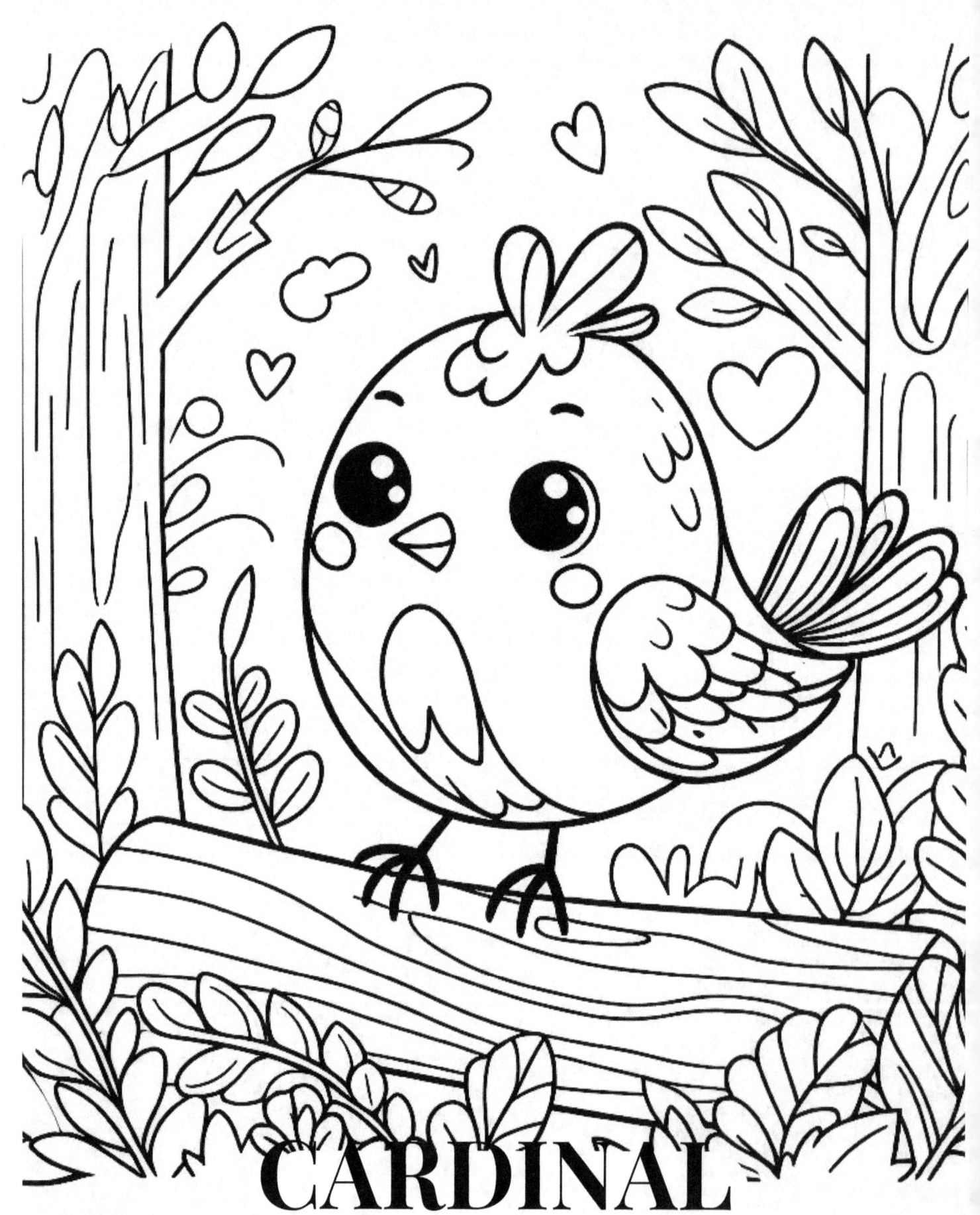

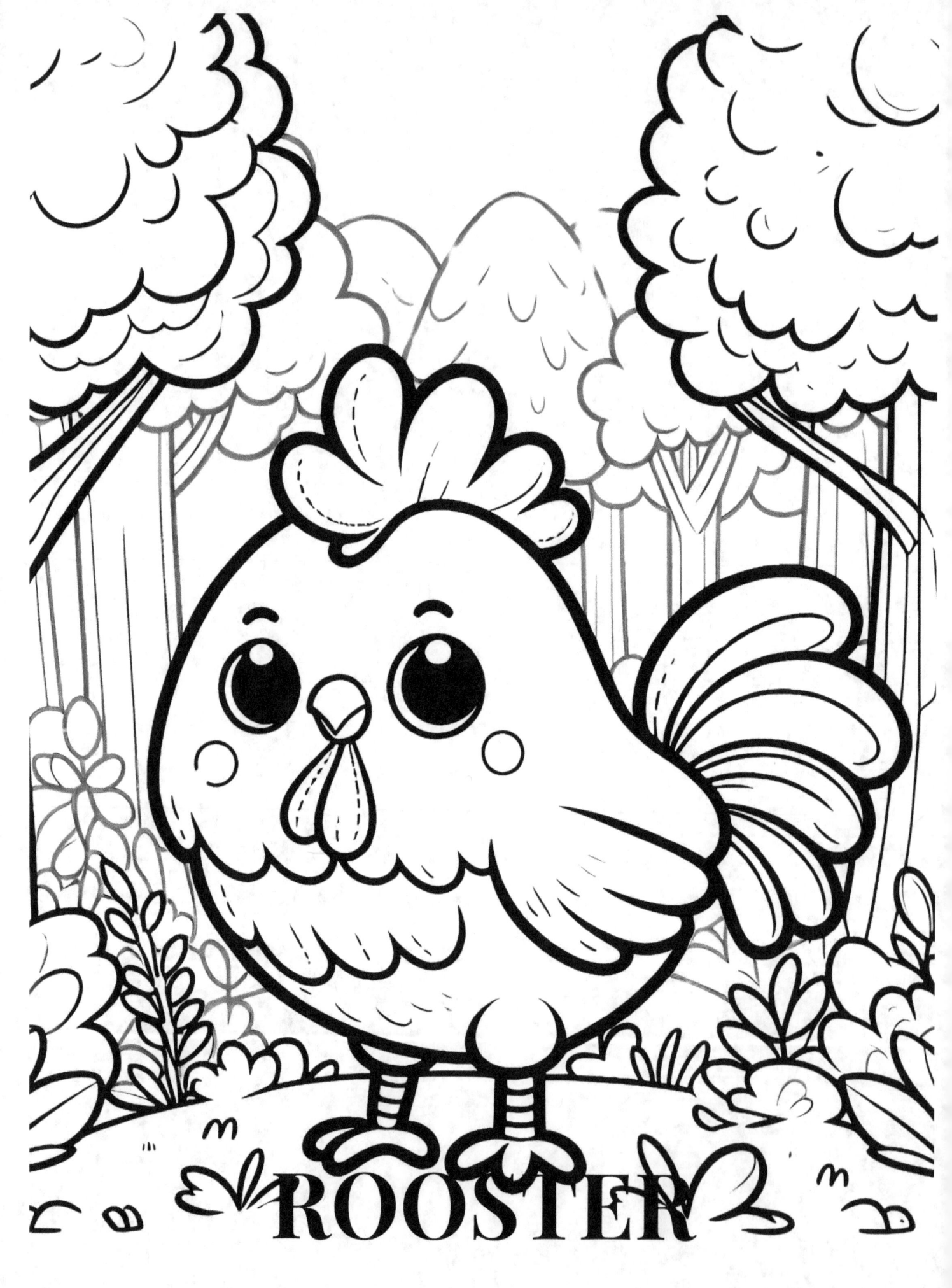

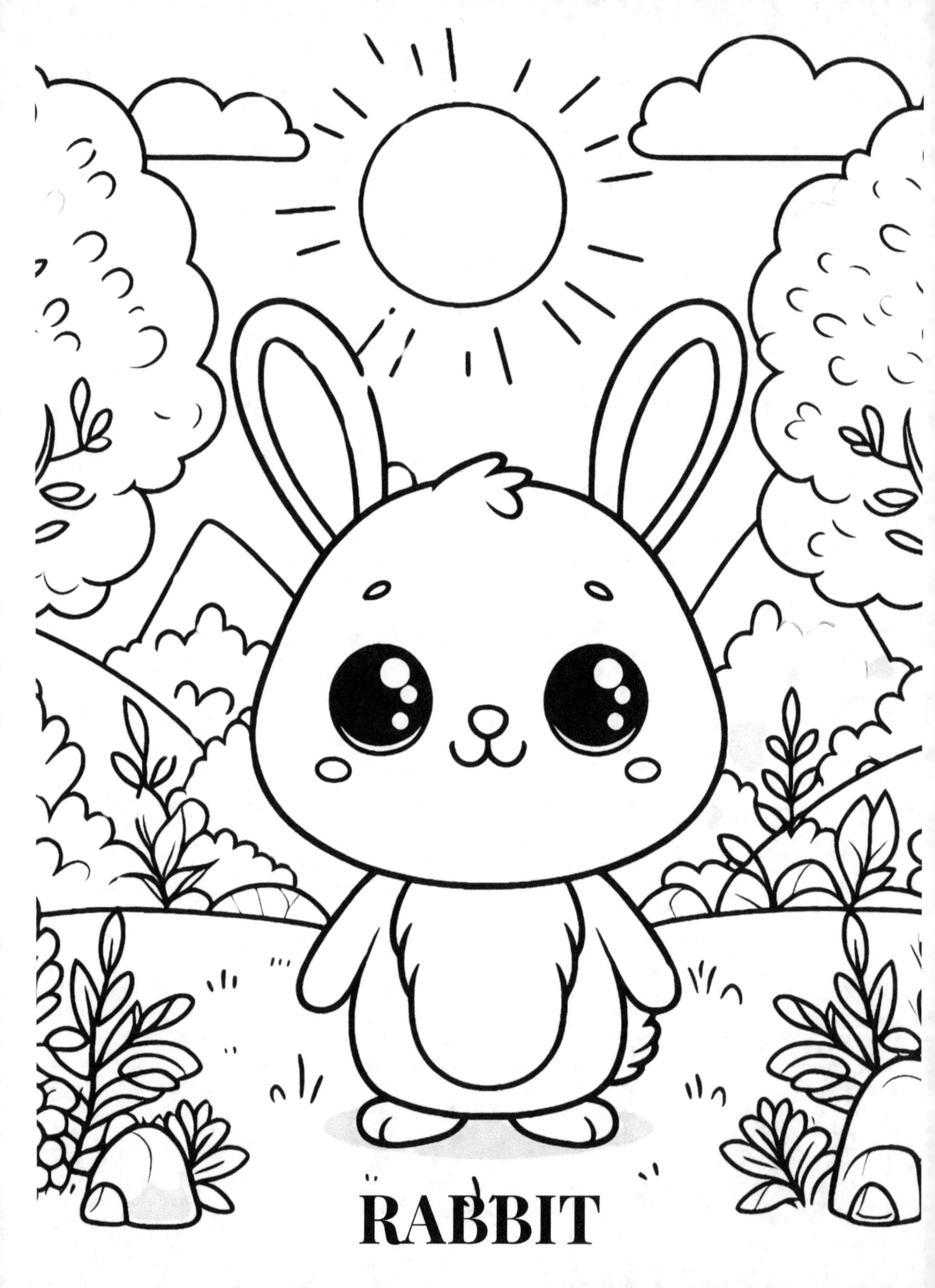

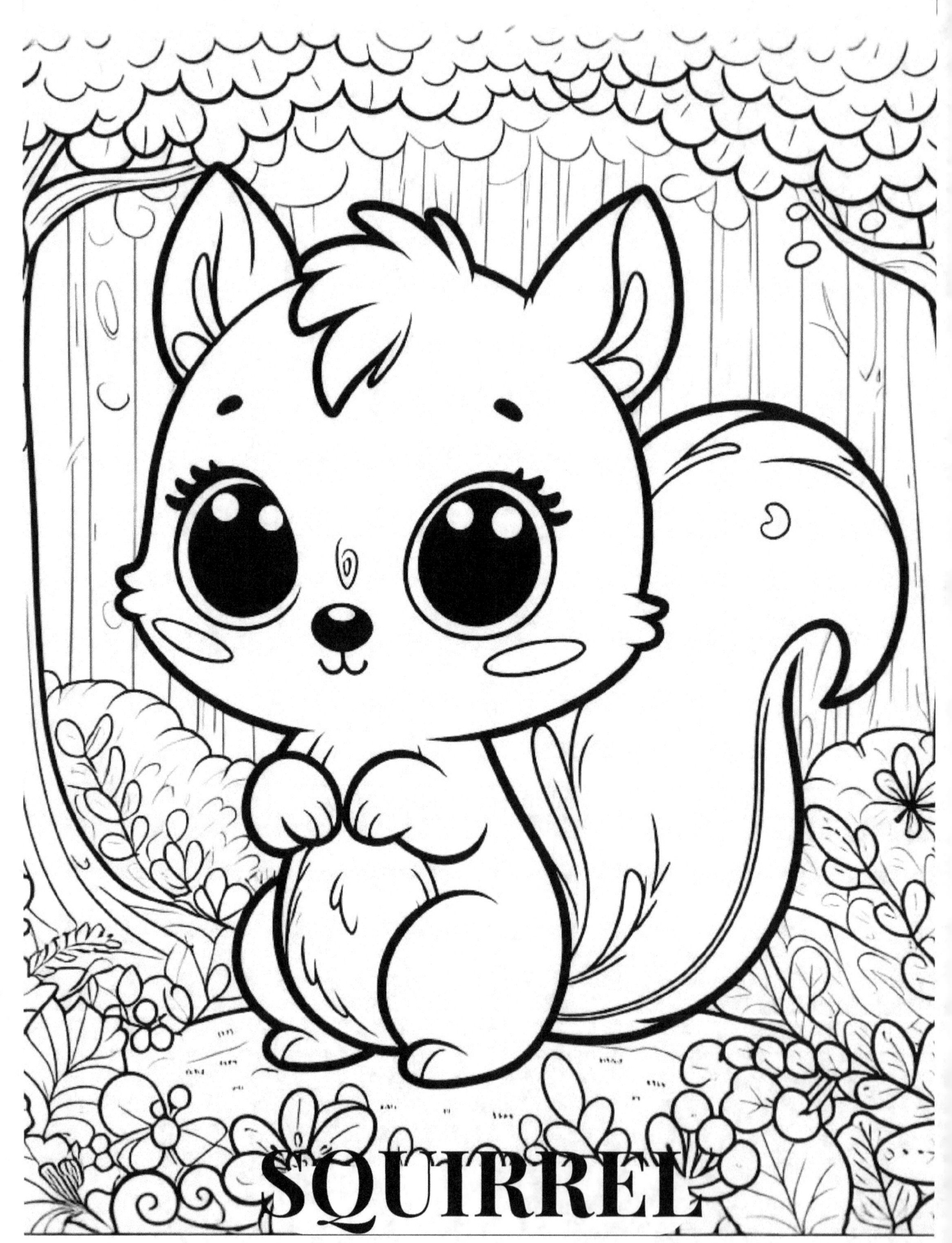

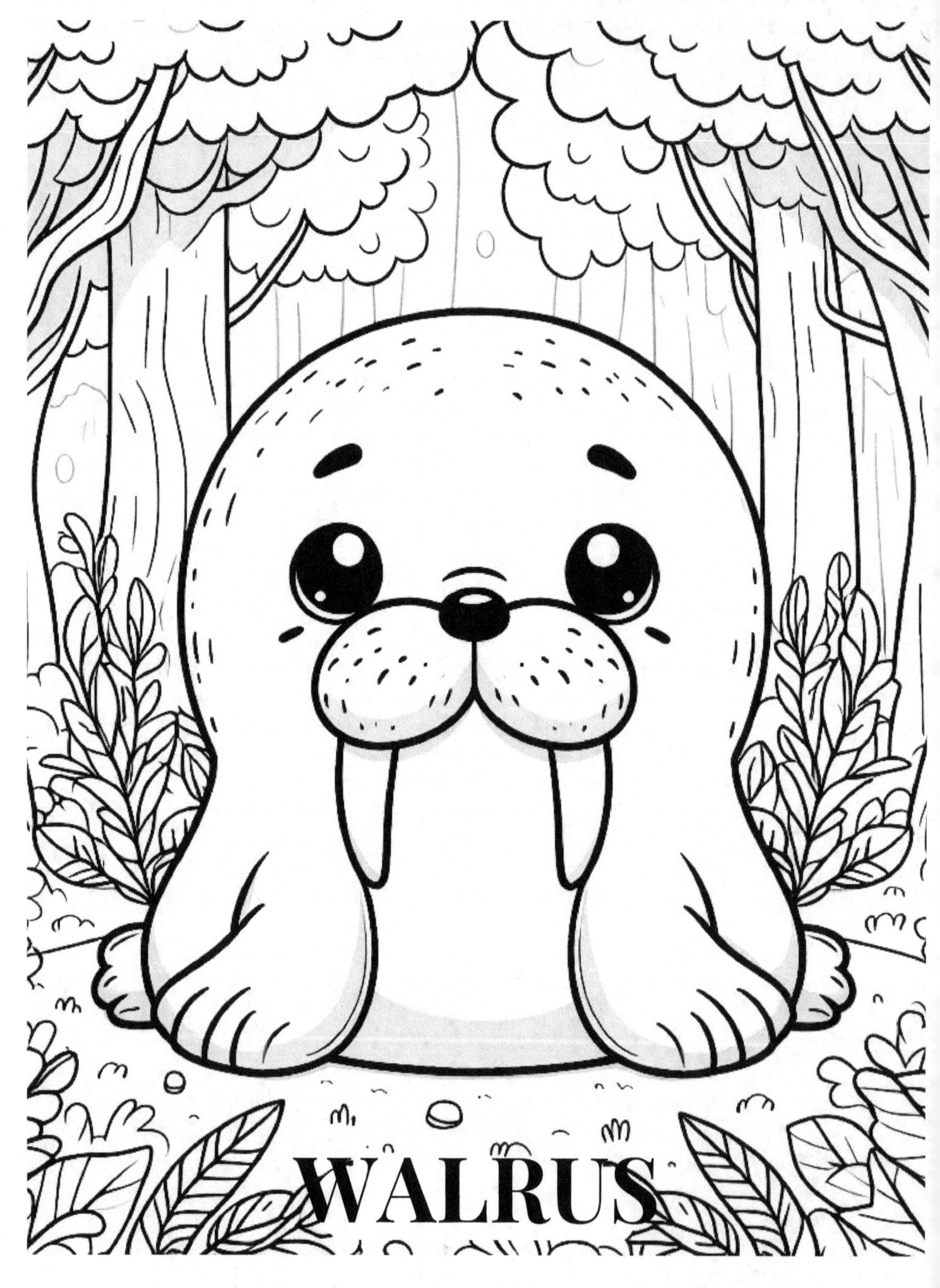

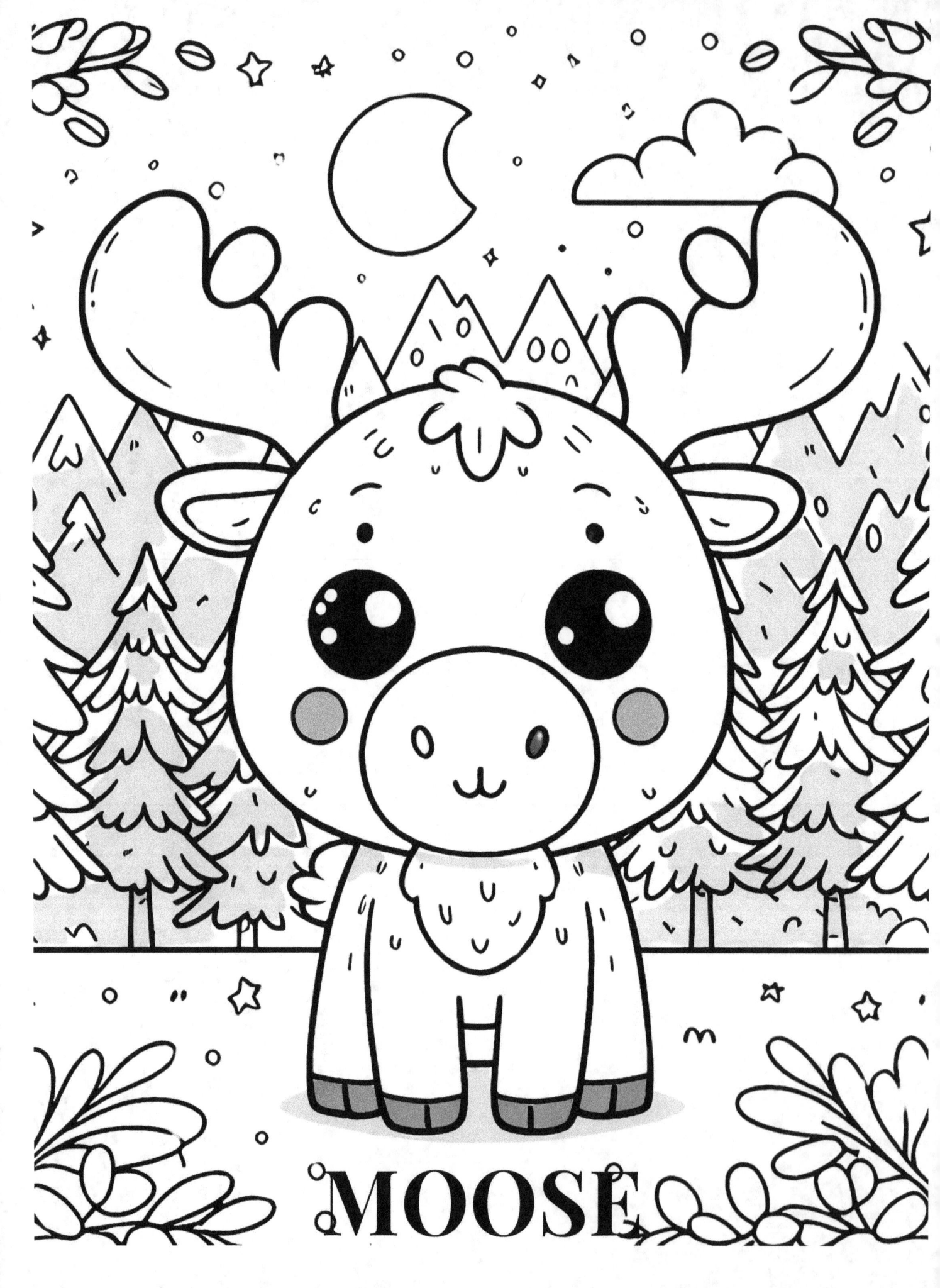

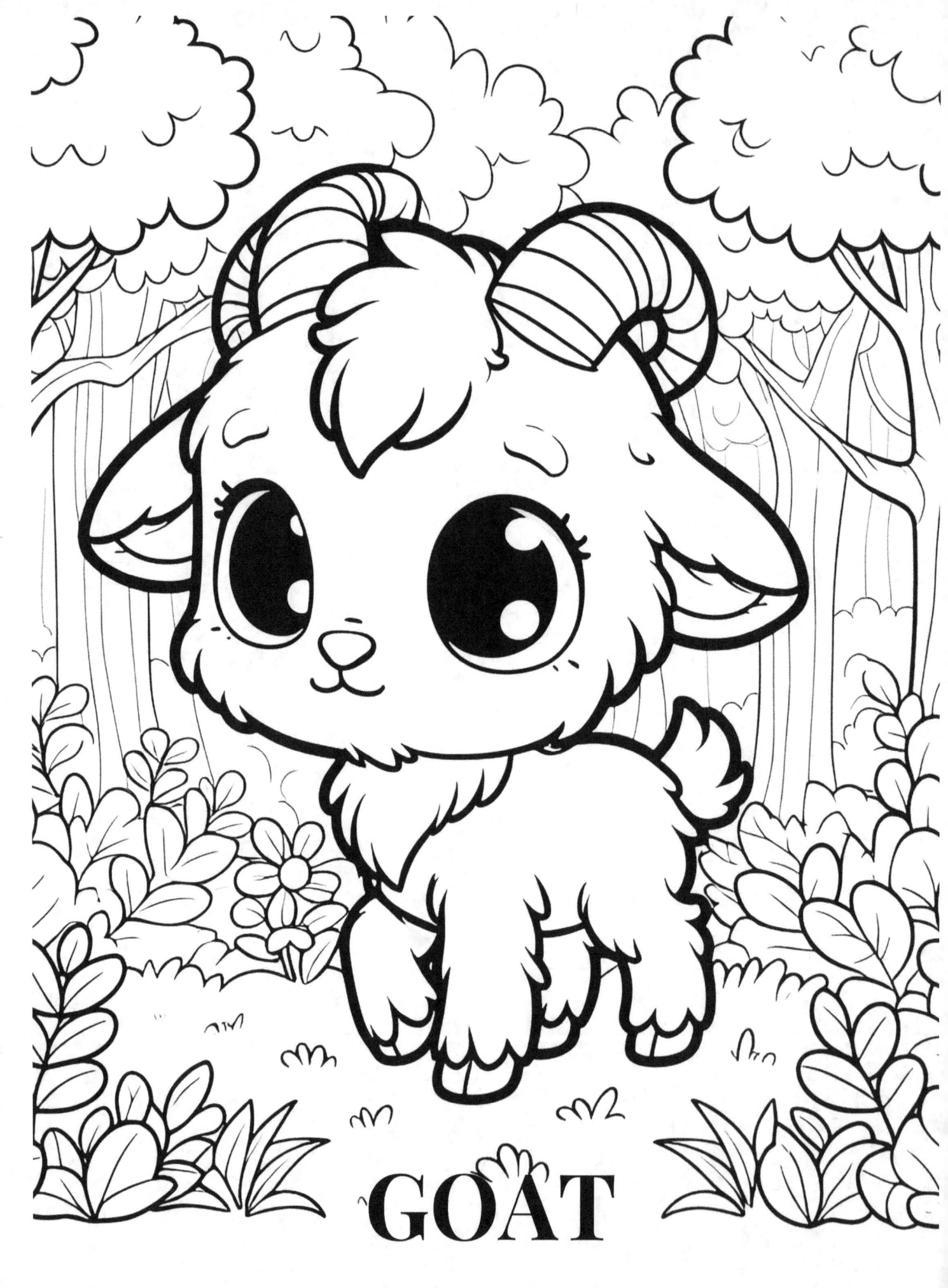

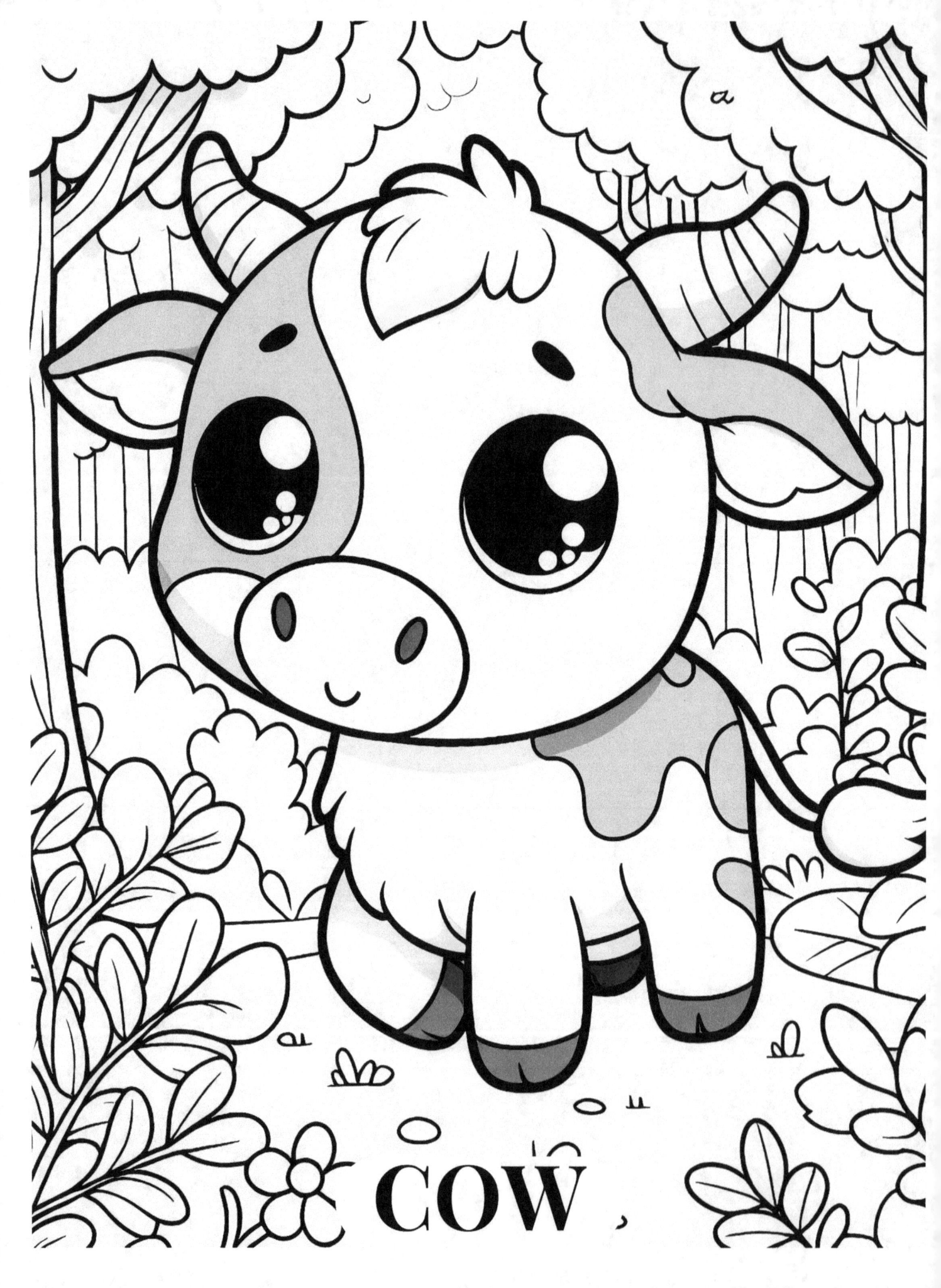

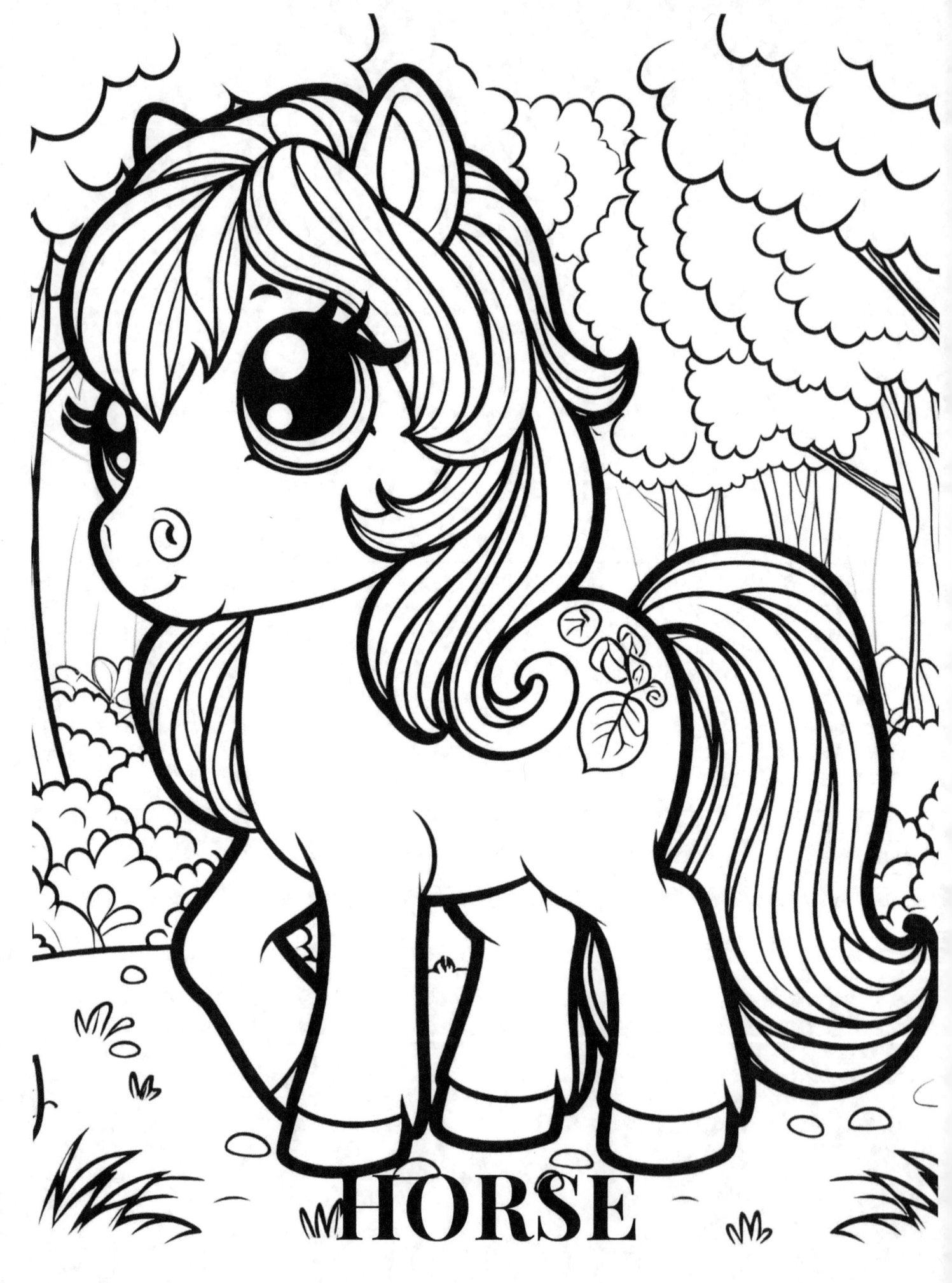

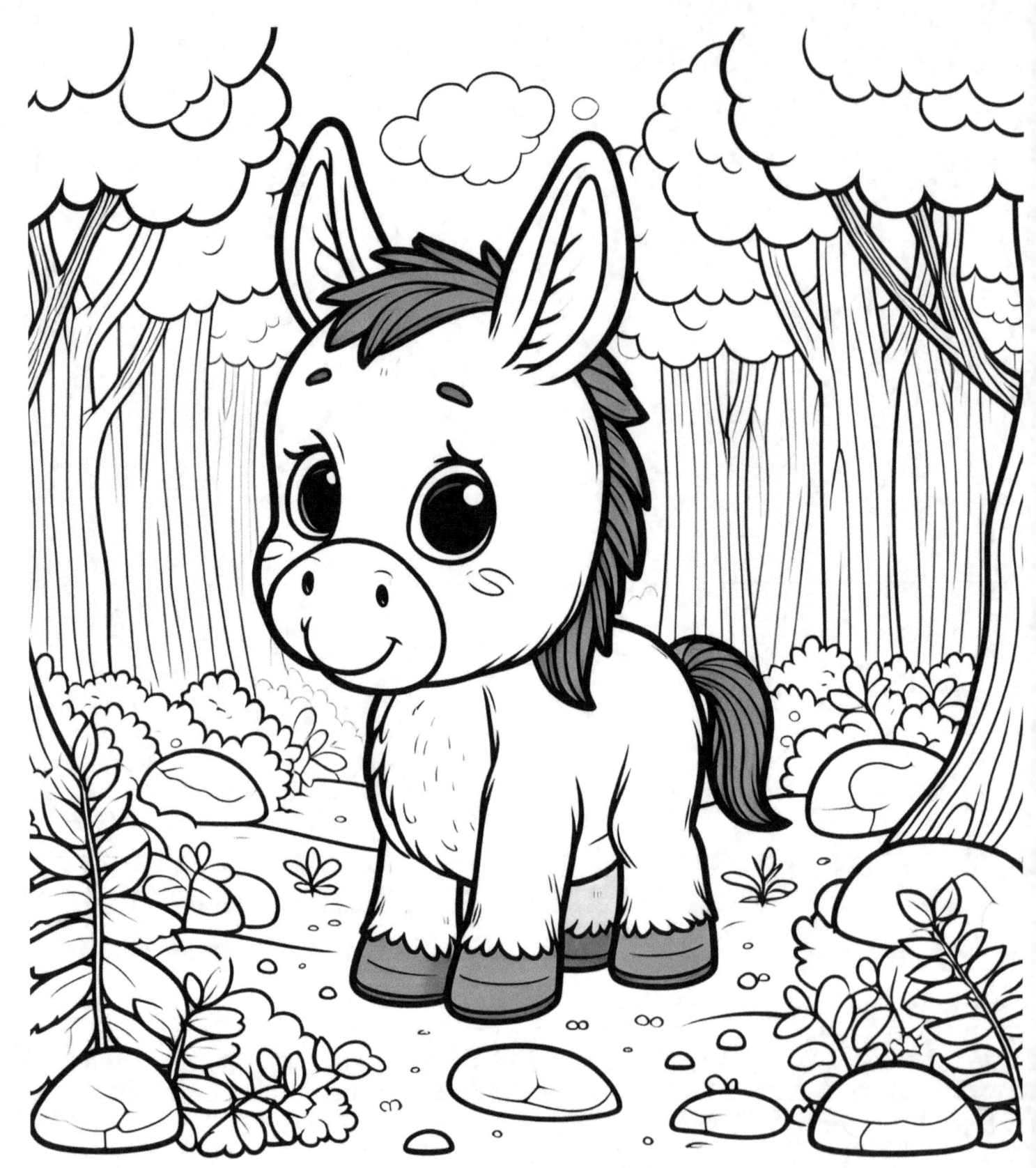

DUMB

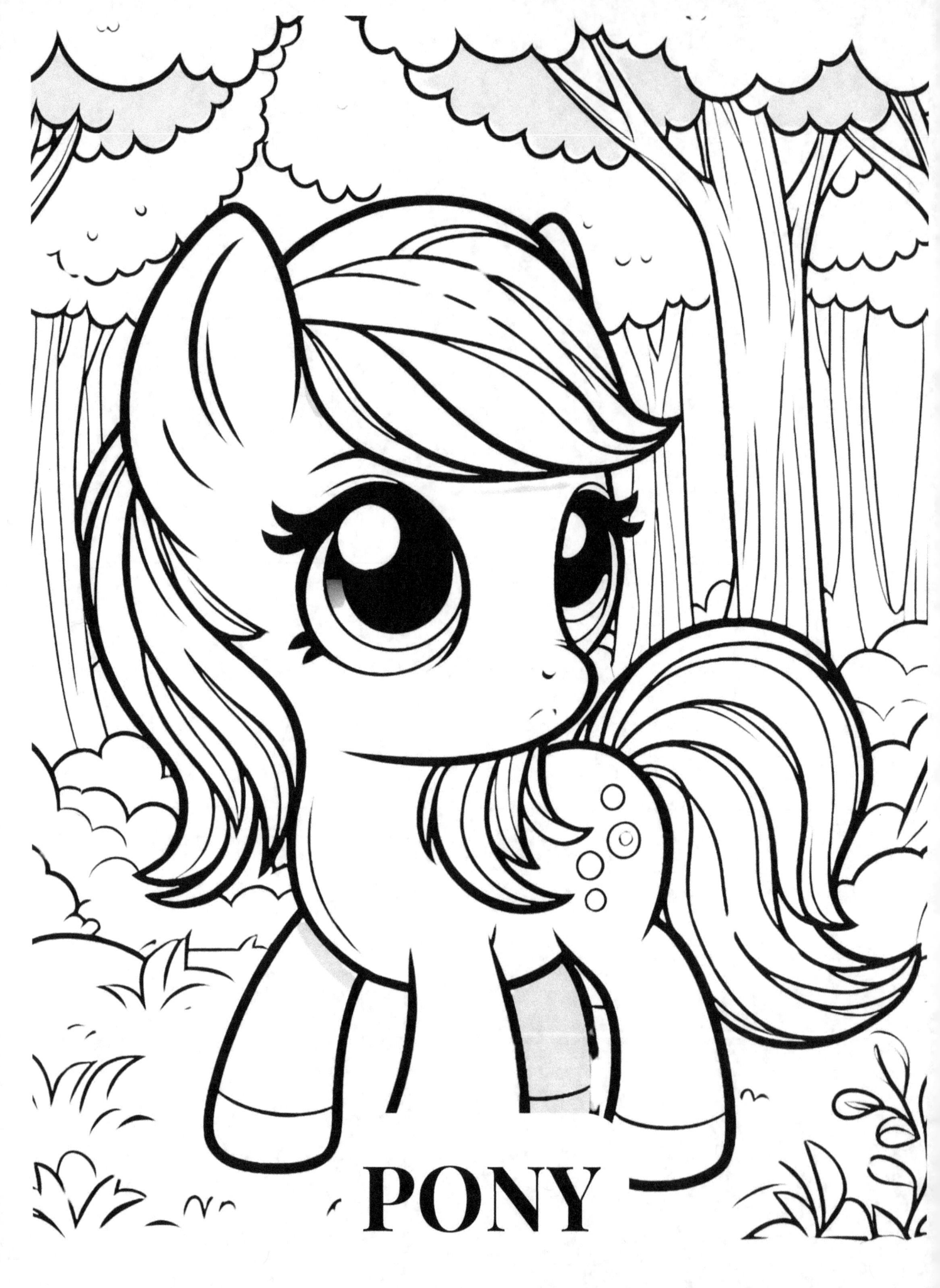

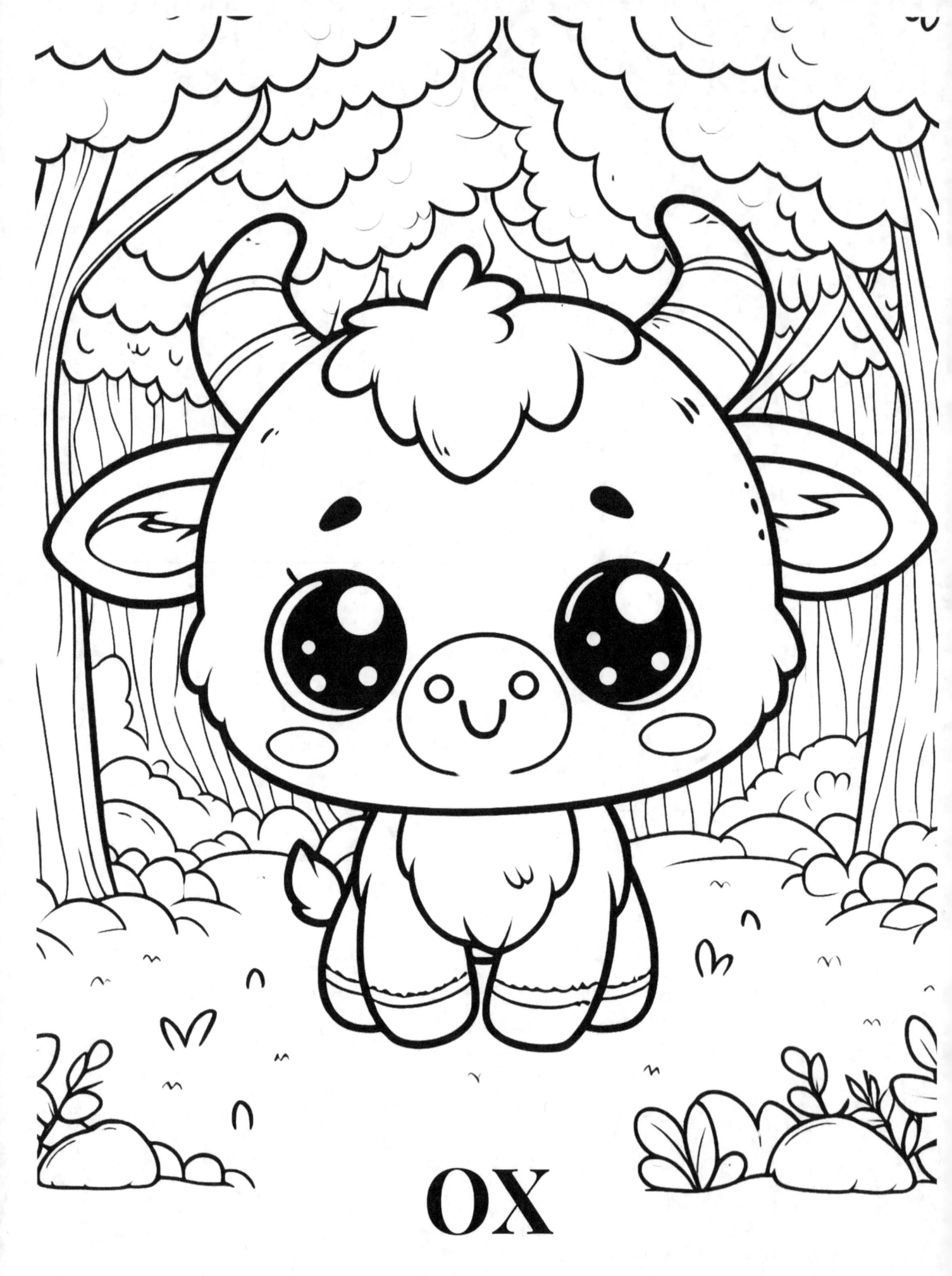

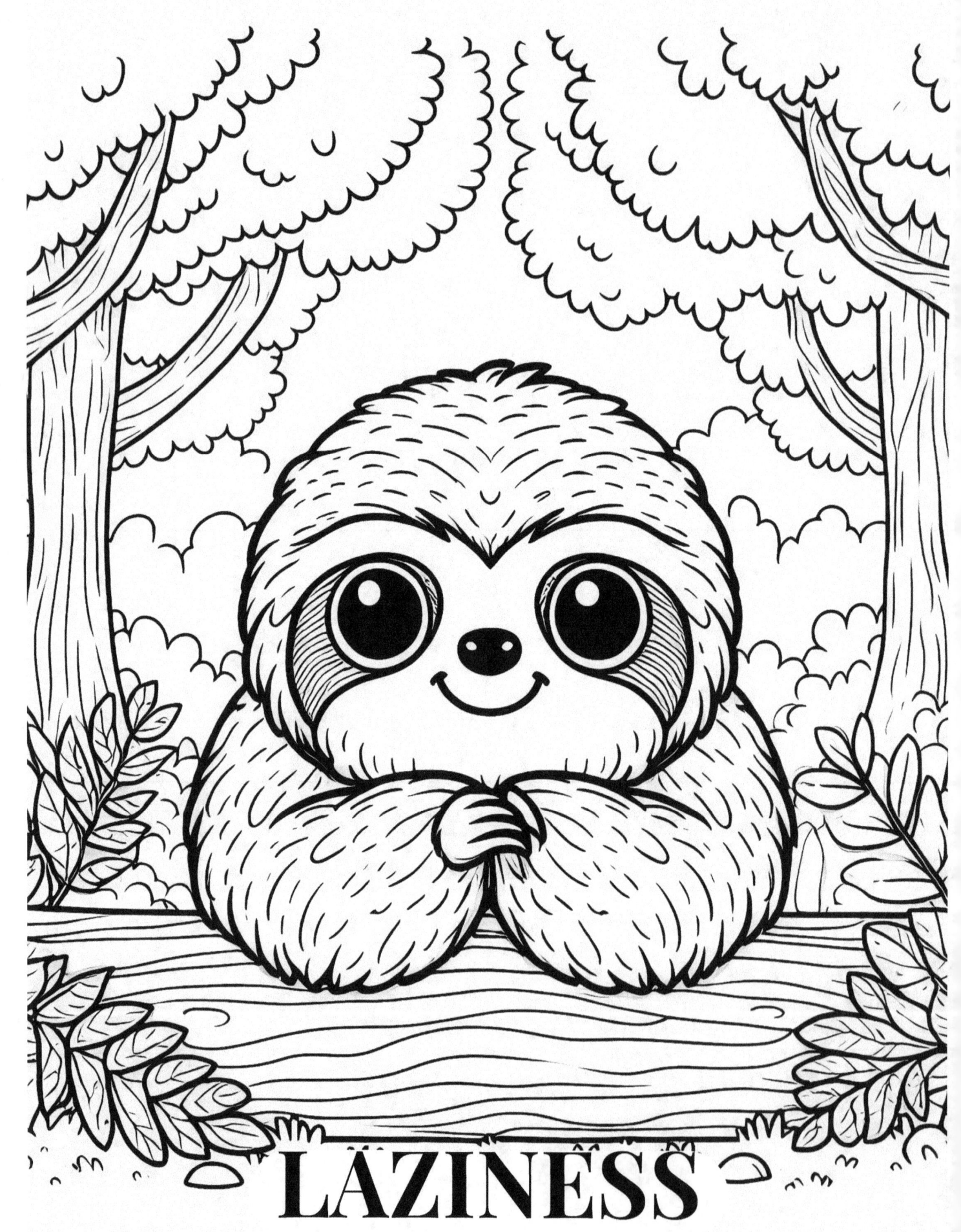

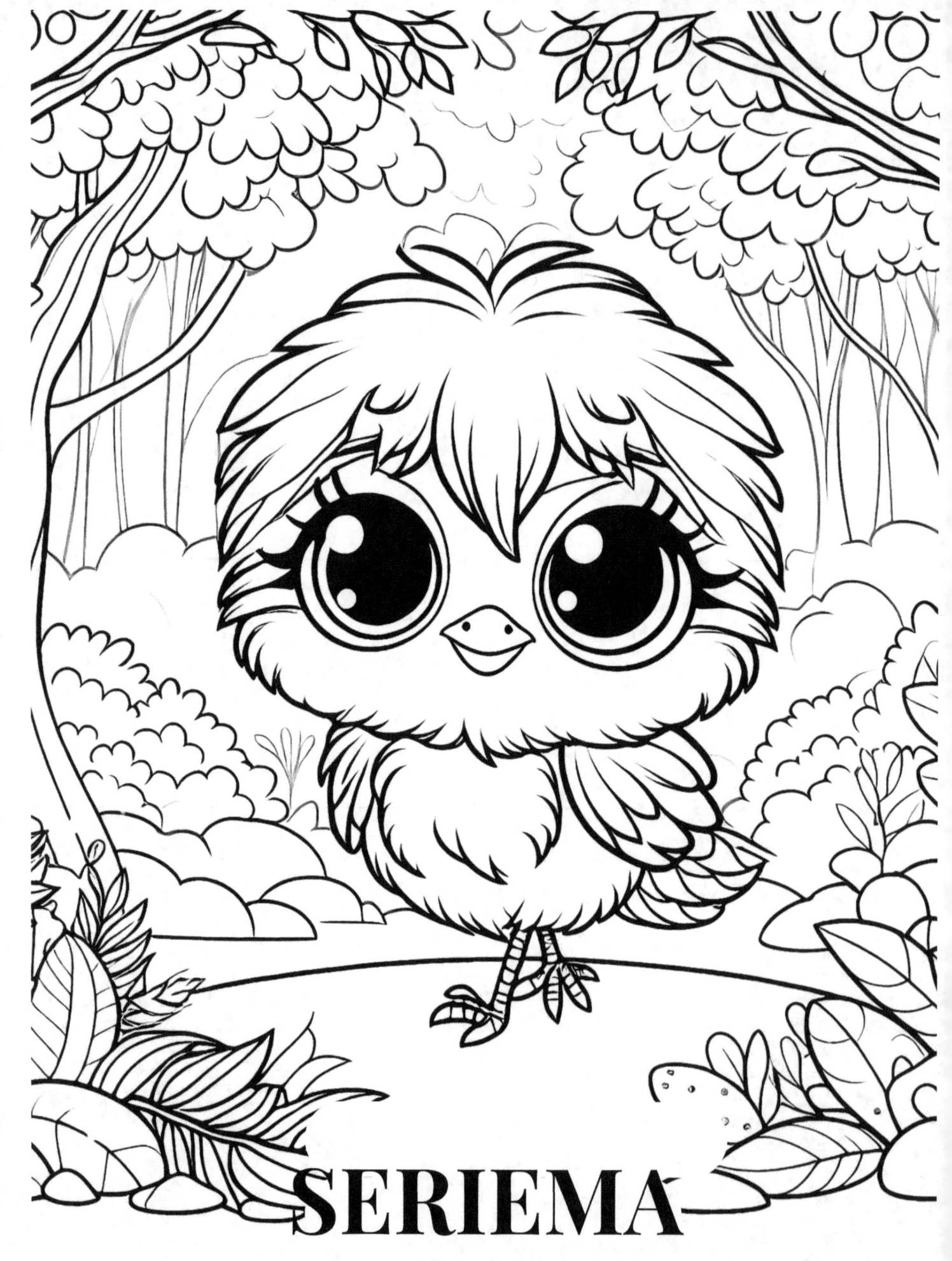

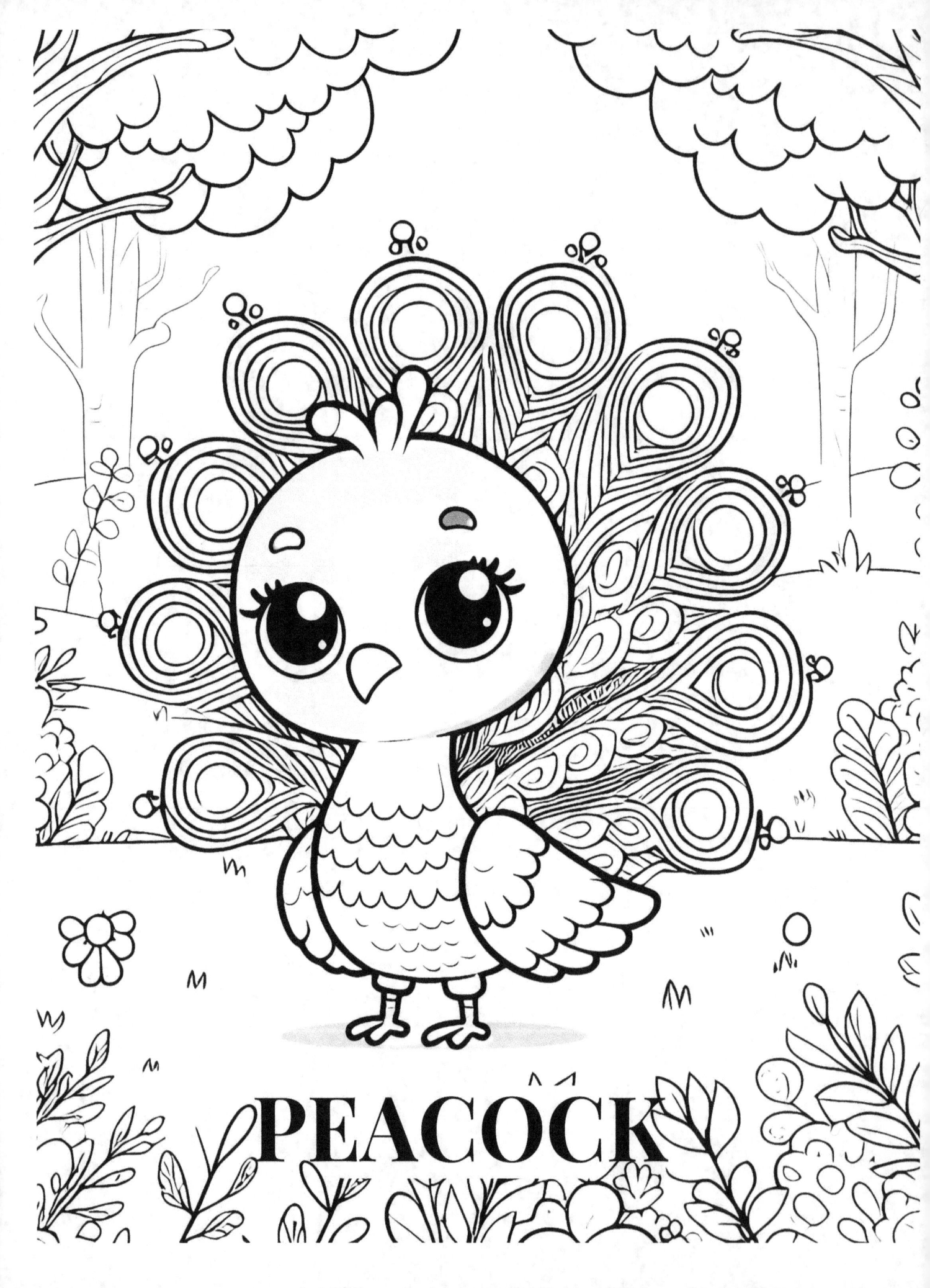

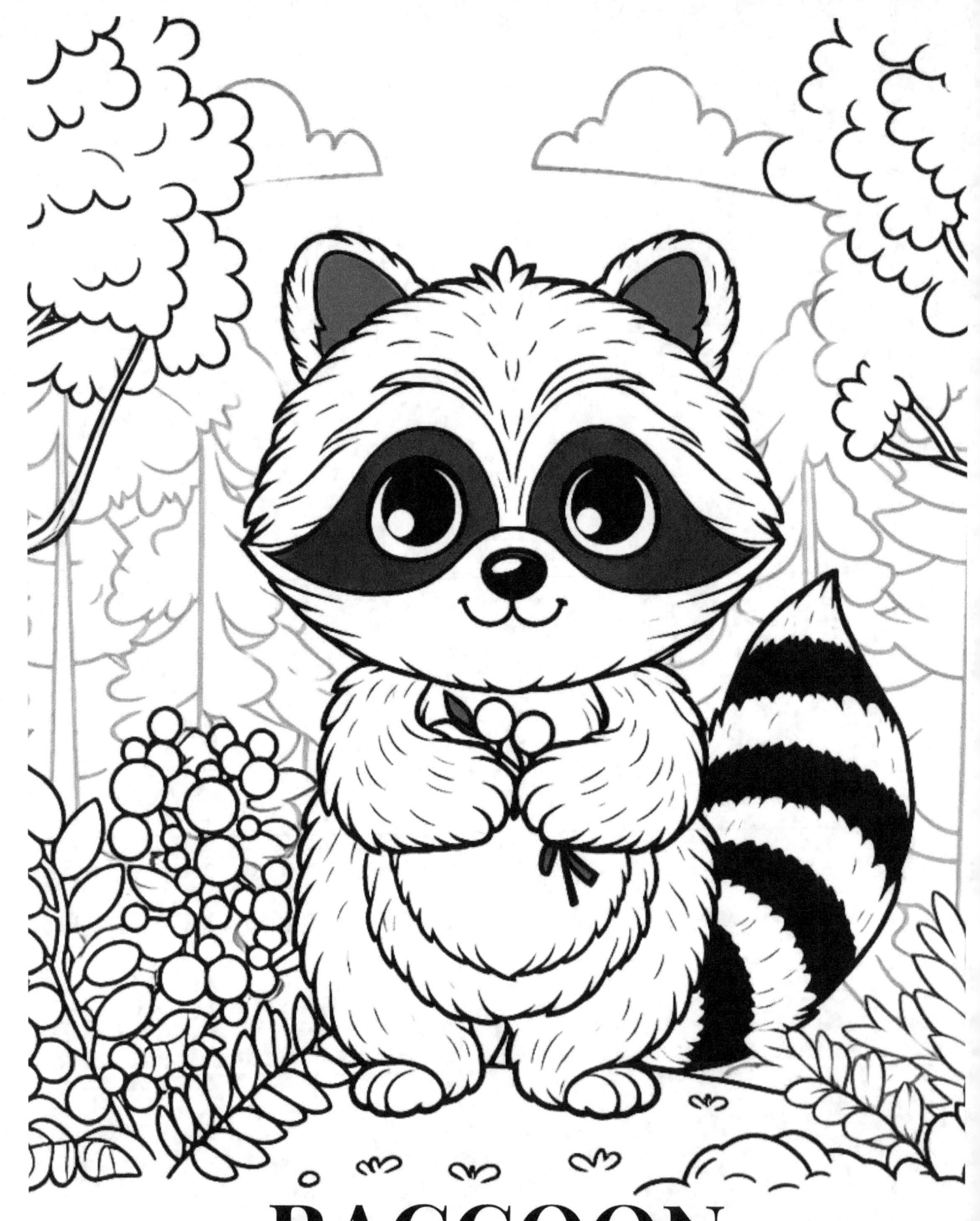

RACCOON

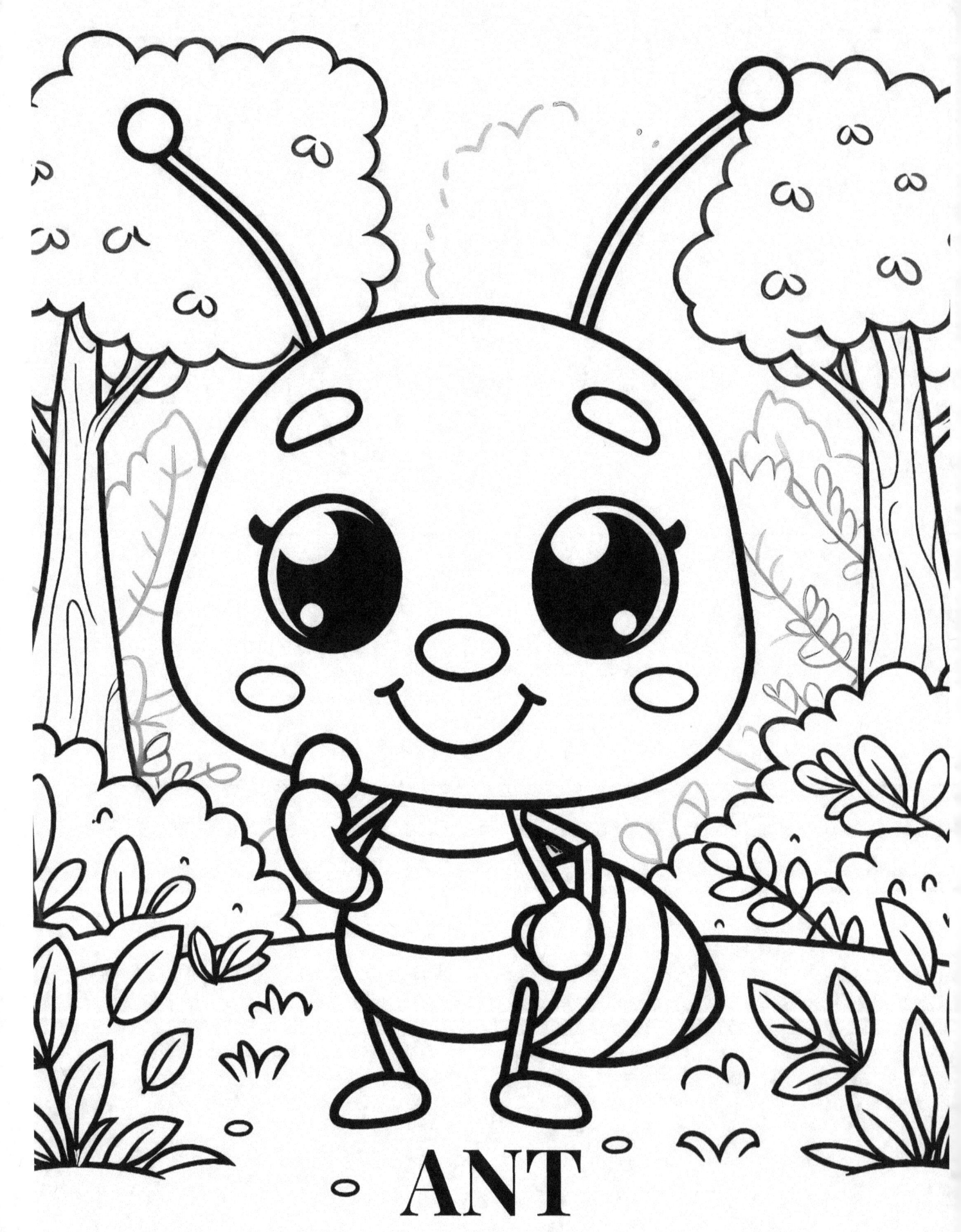

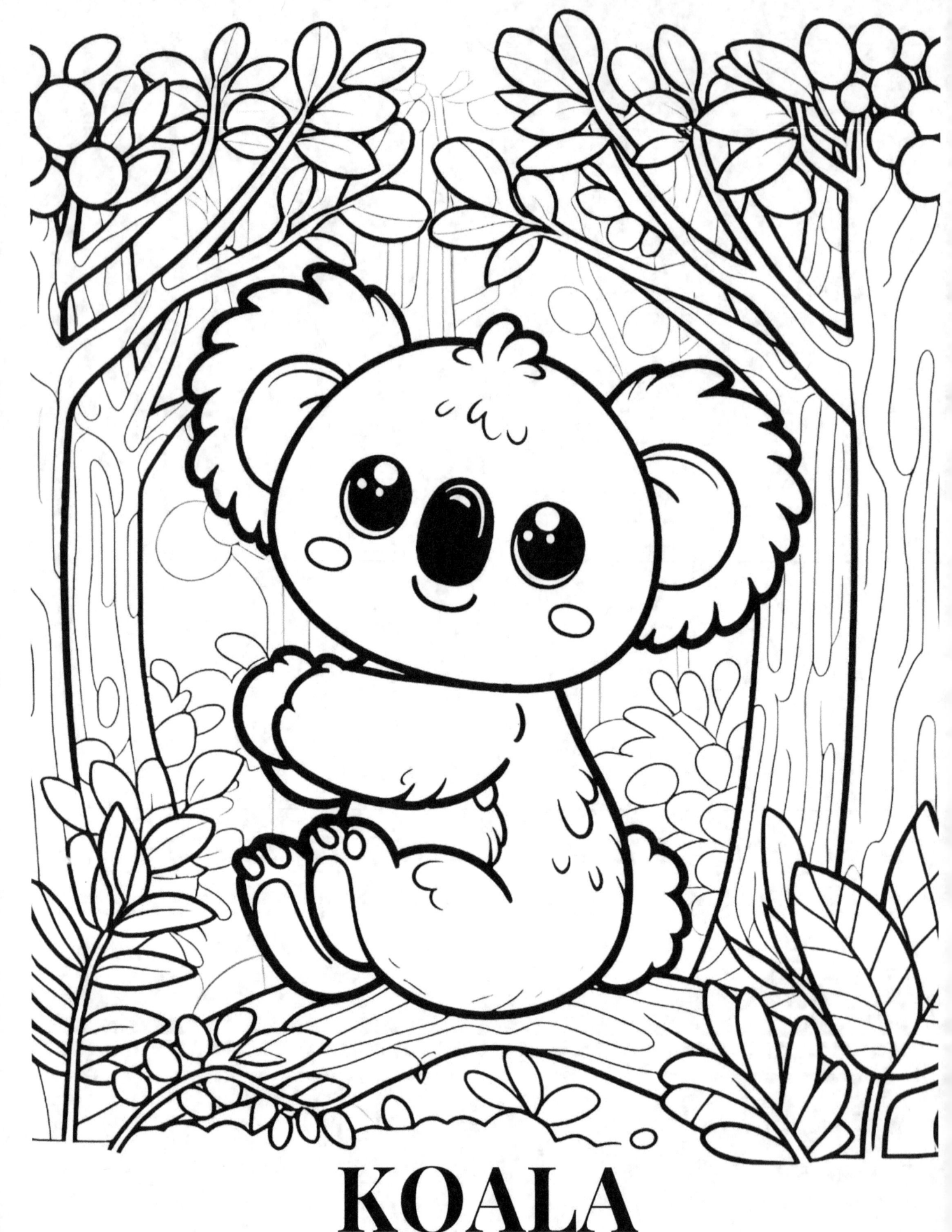

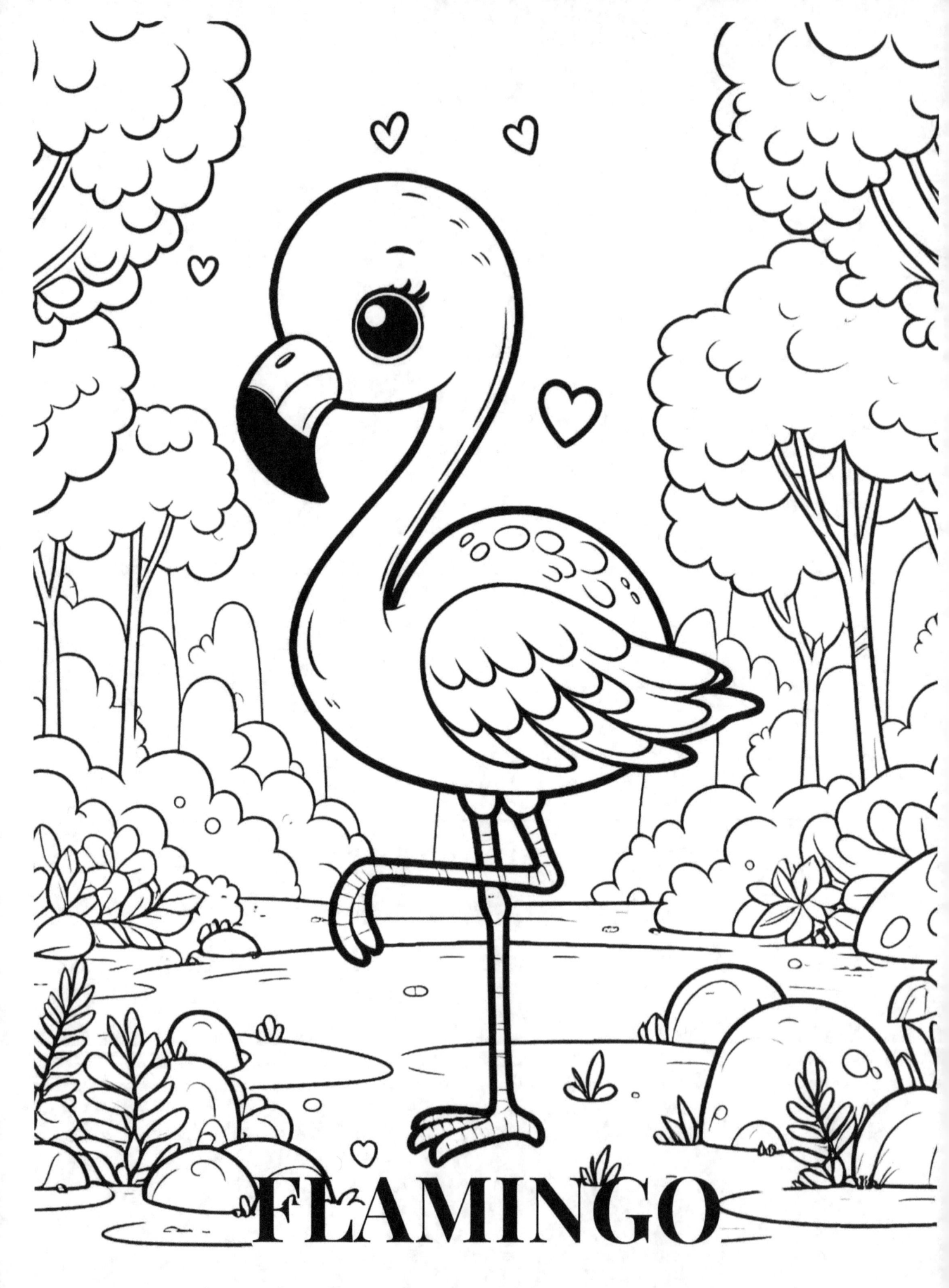

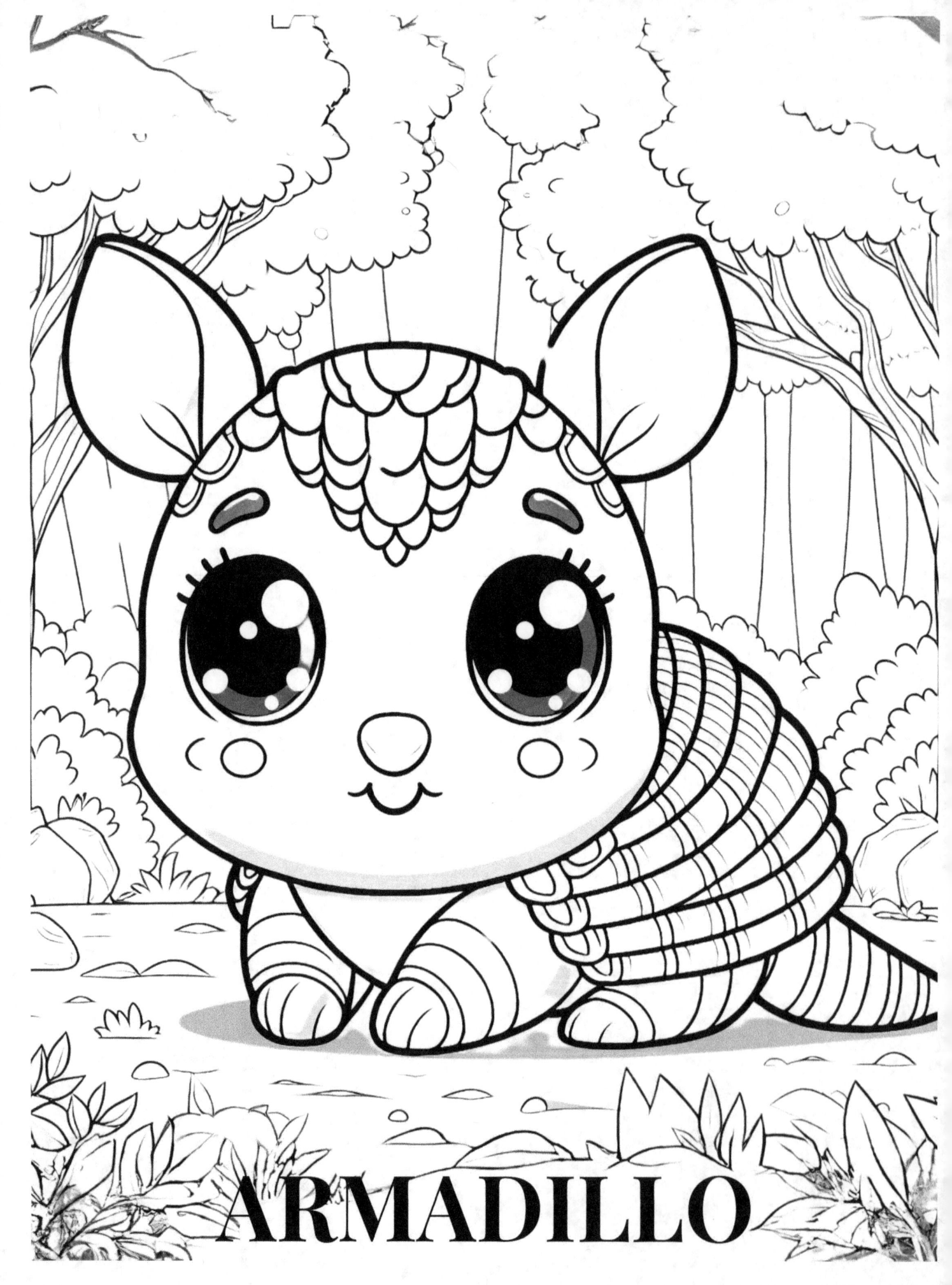

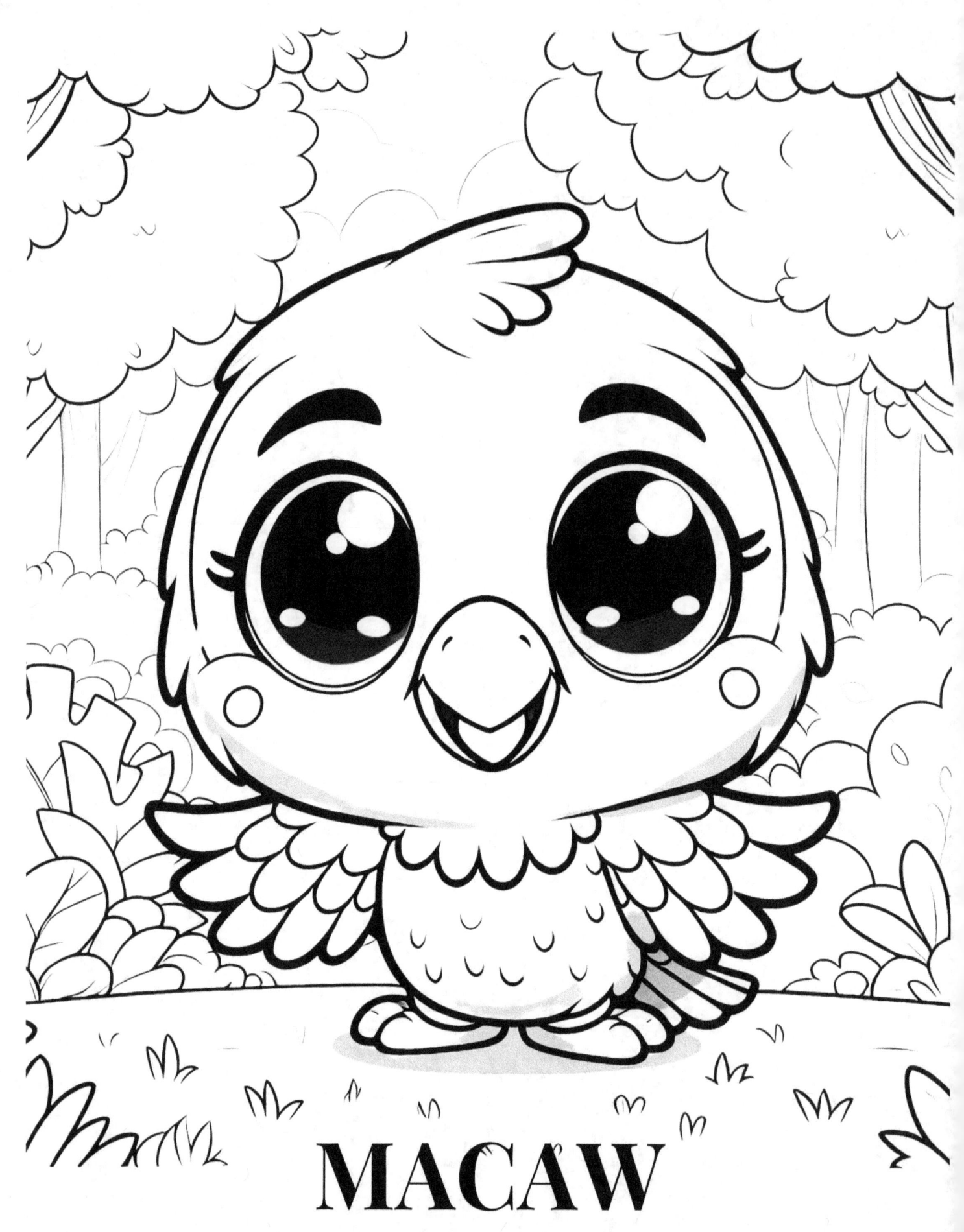

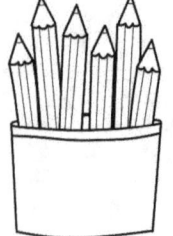 **To Paint**

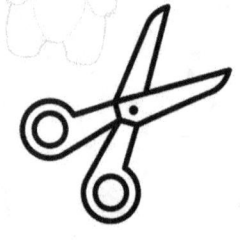 **To Cut Out**
(Ask an adult for help)

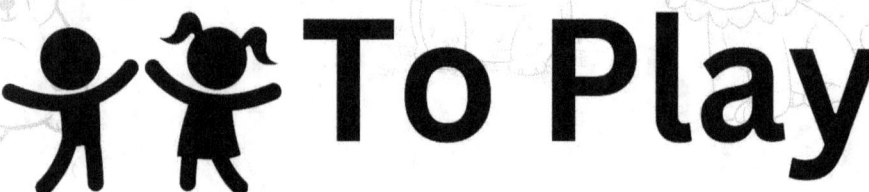 **To Play**

Forest Animals

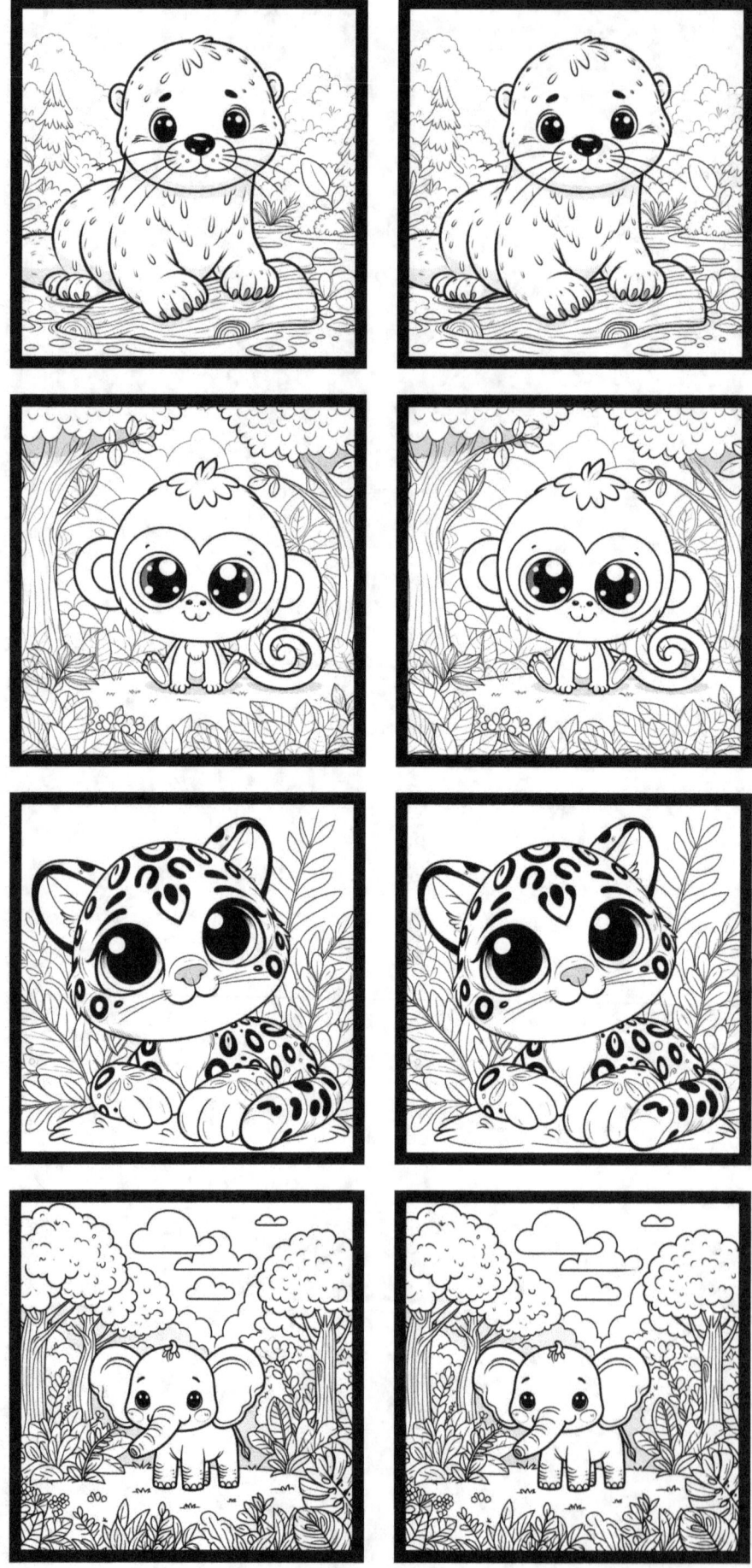

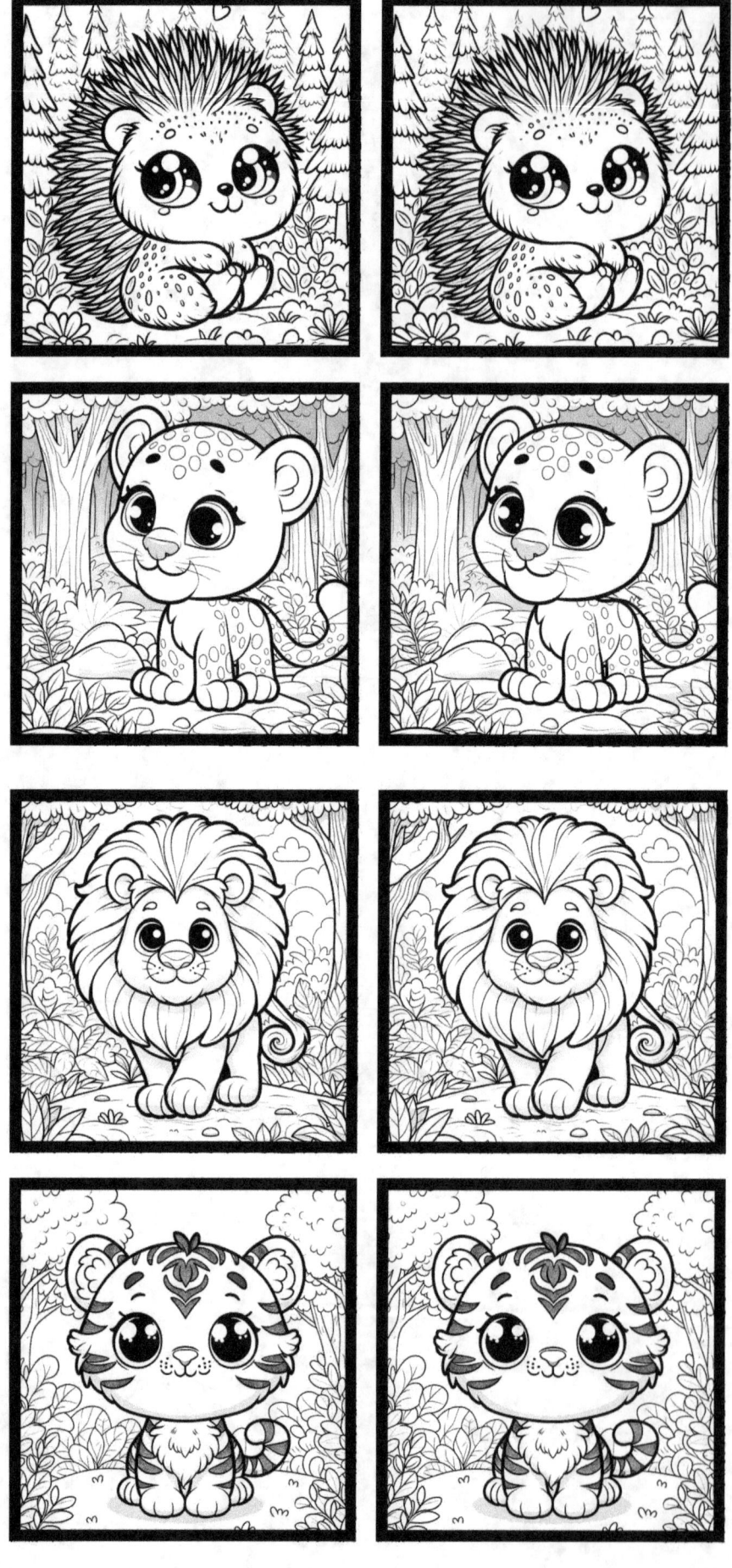

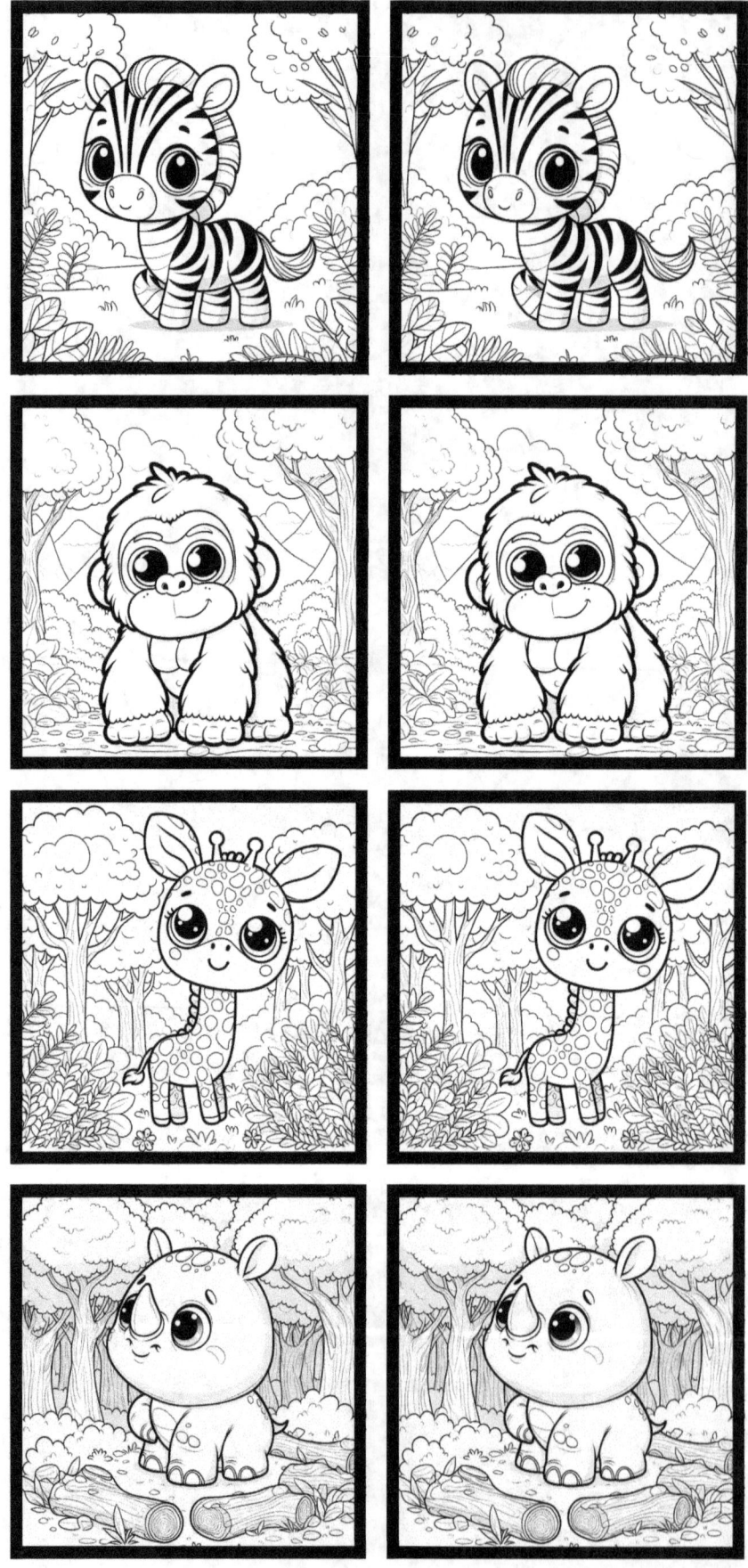

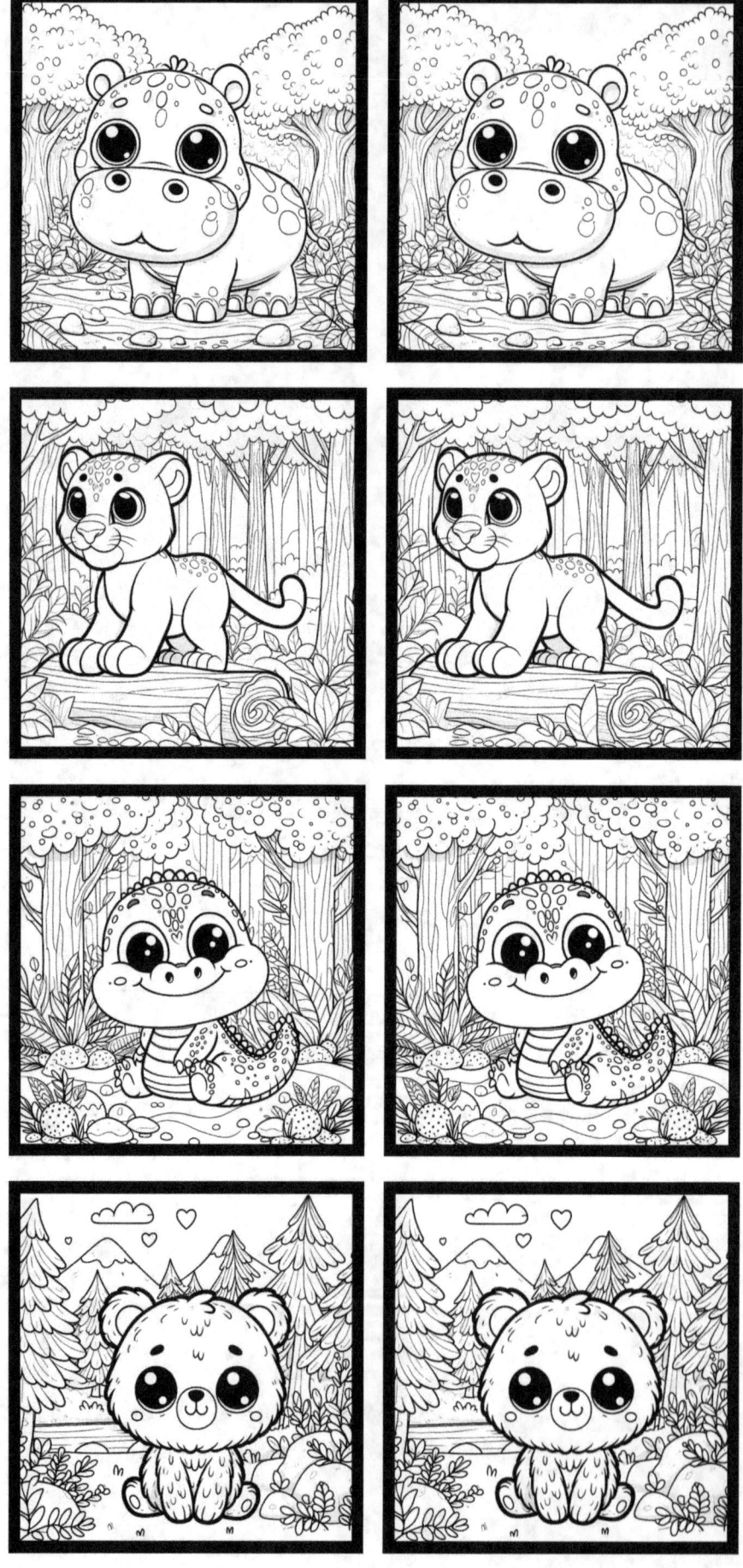

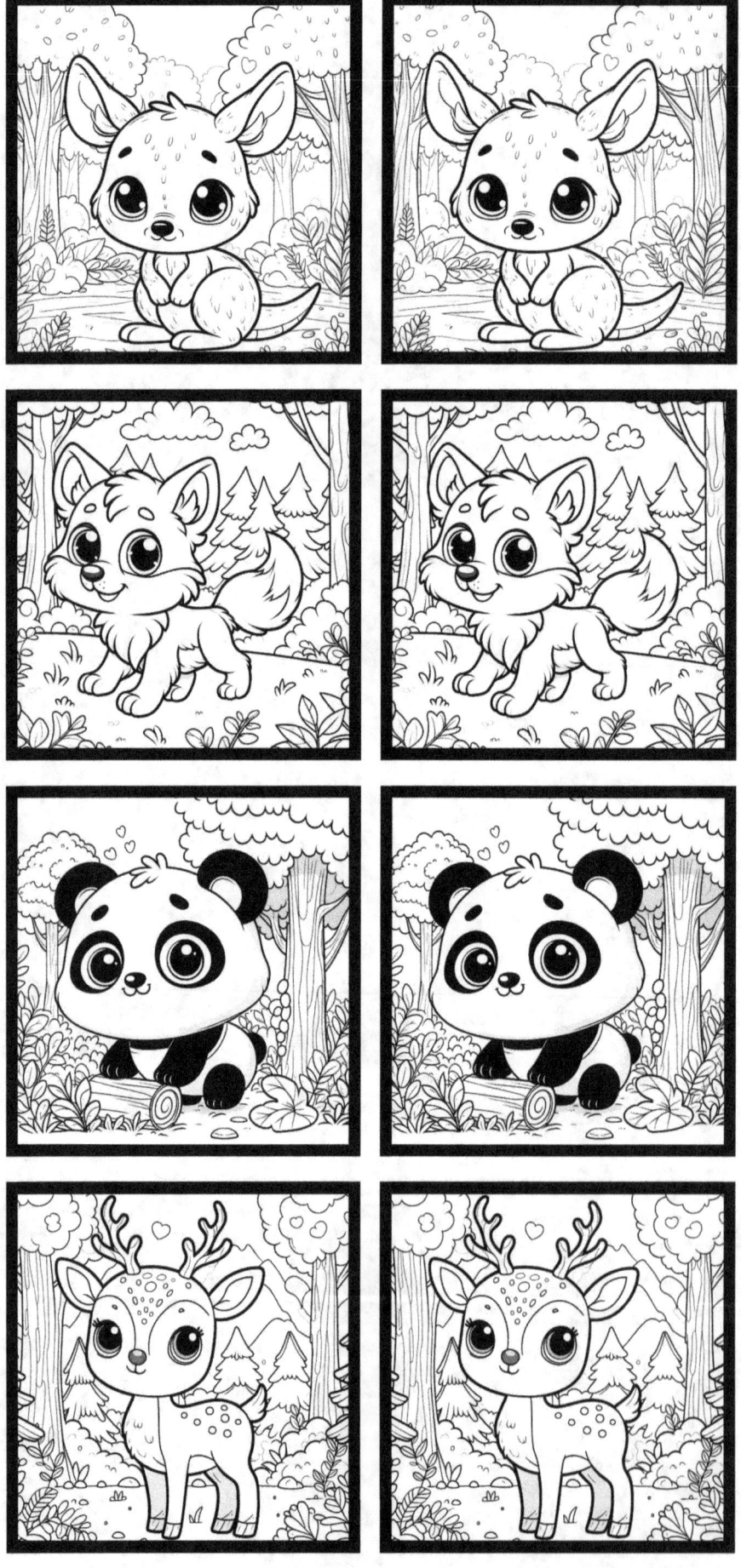

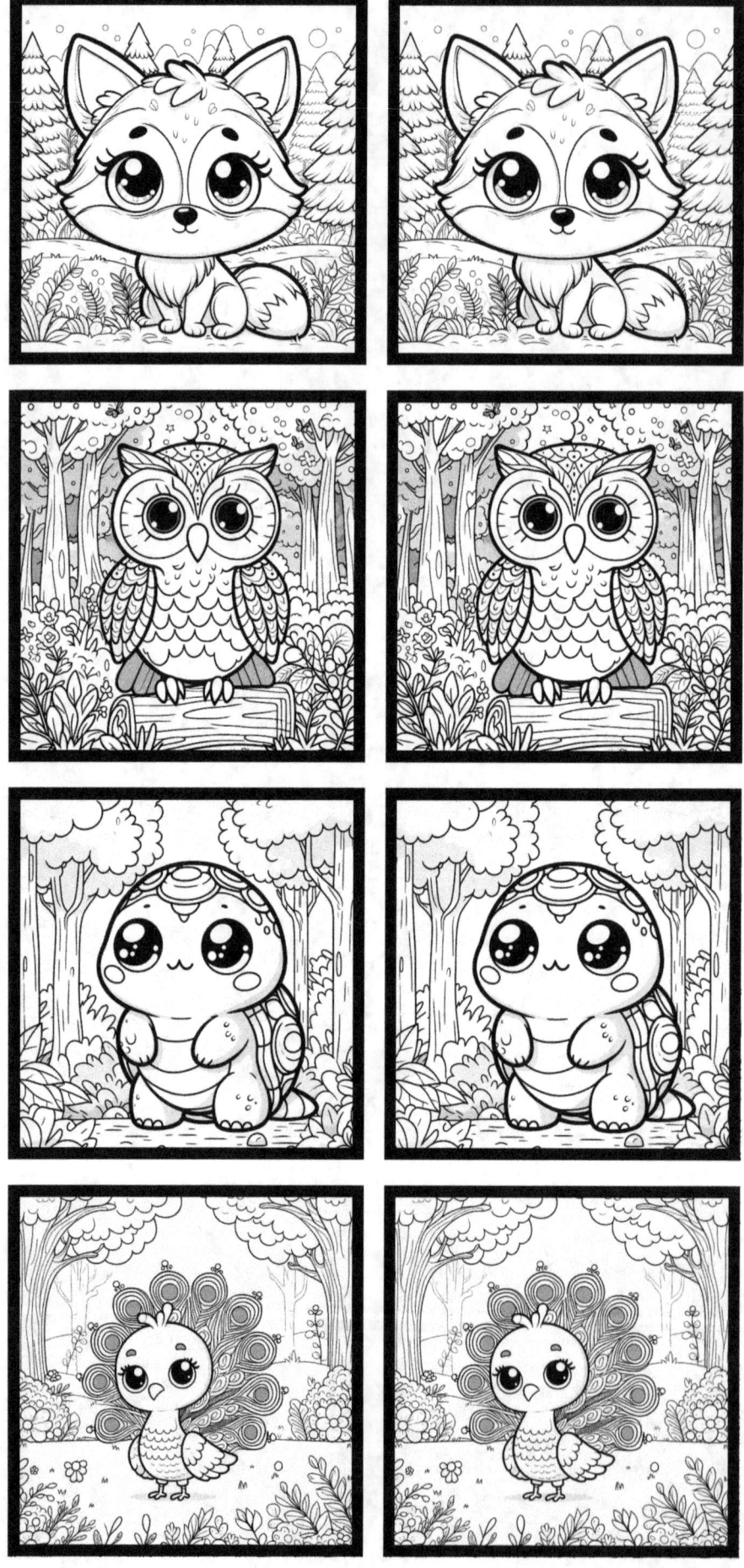

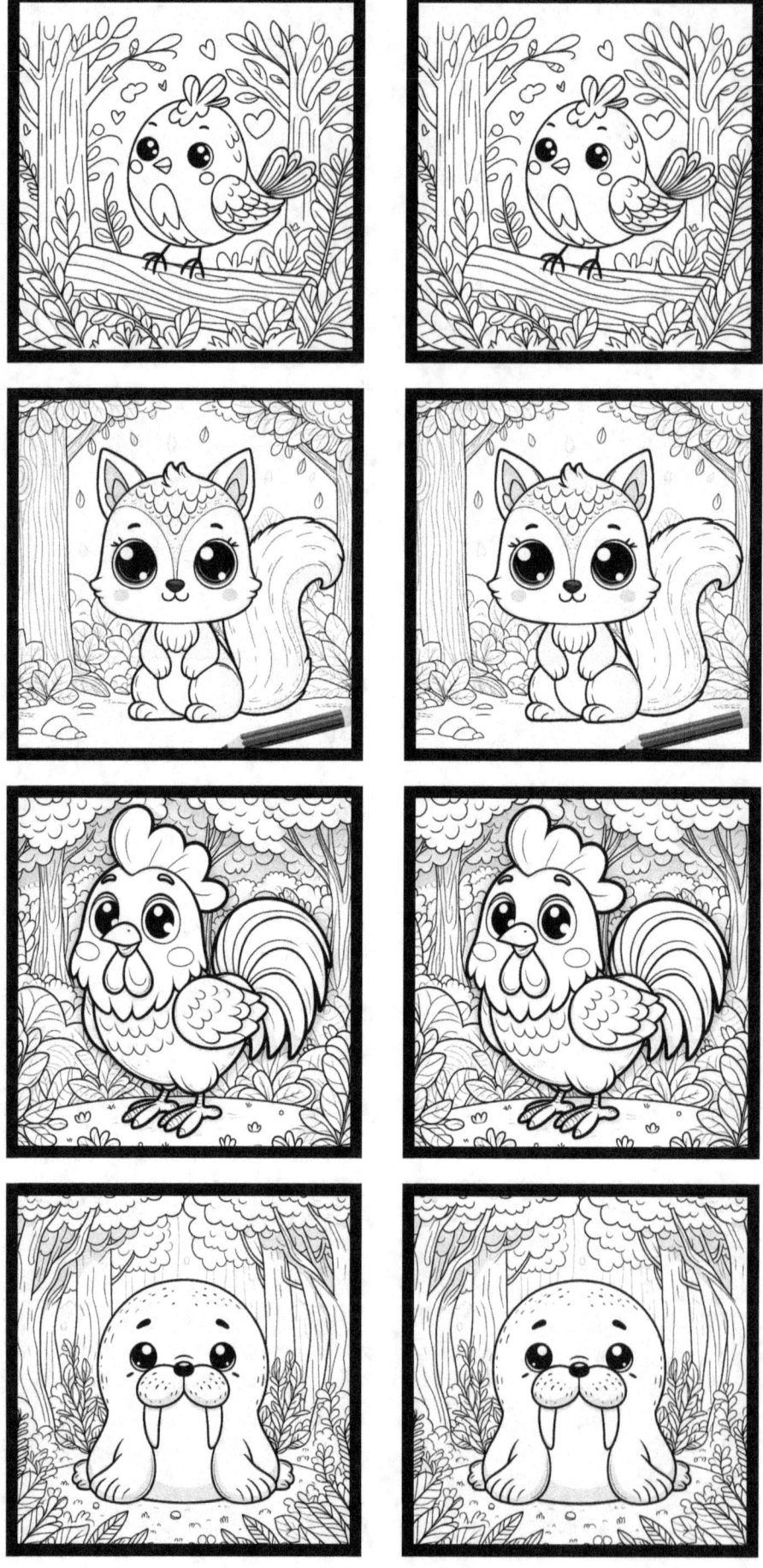

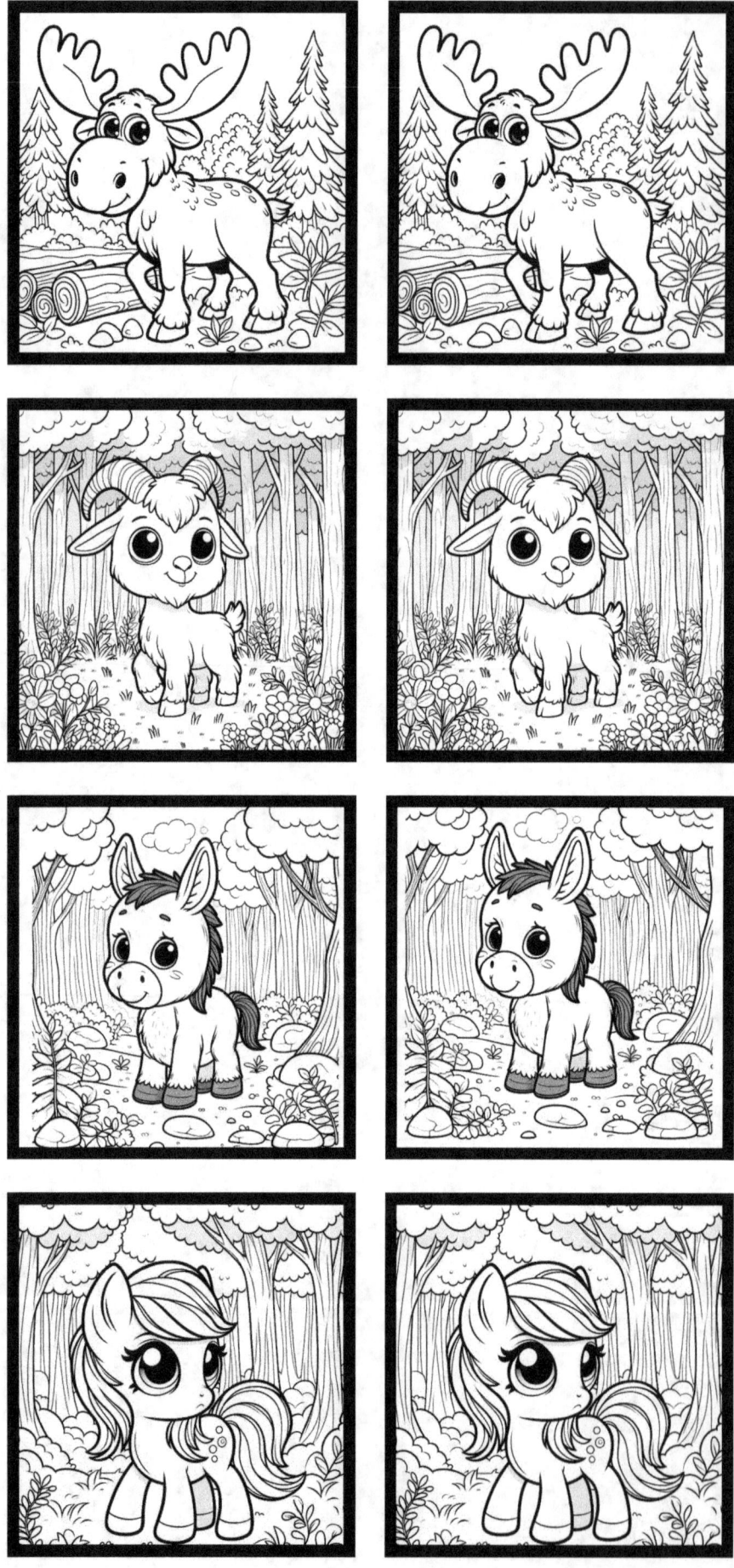

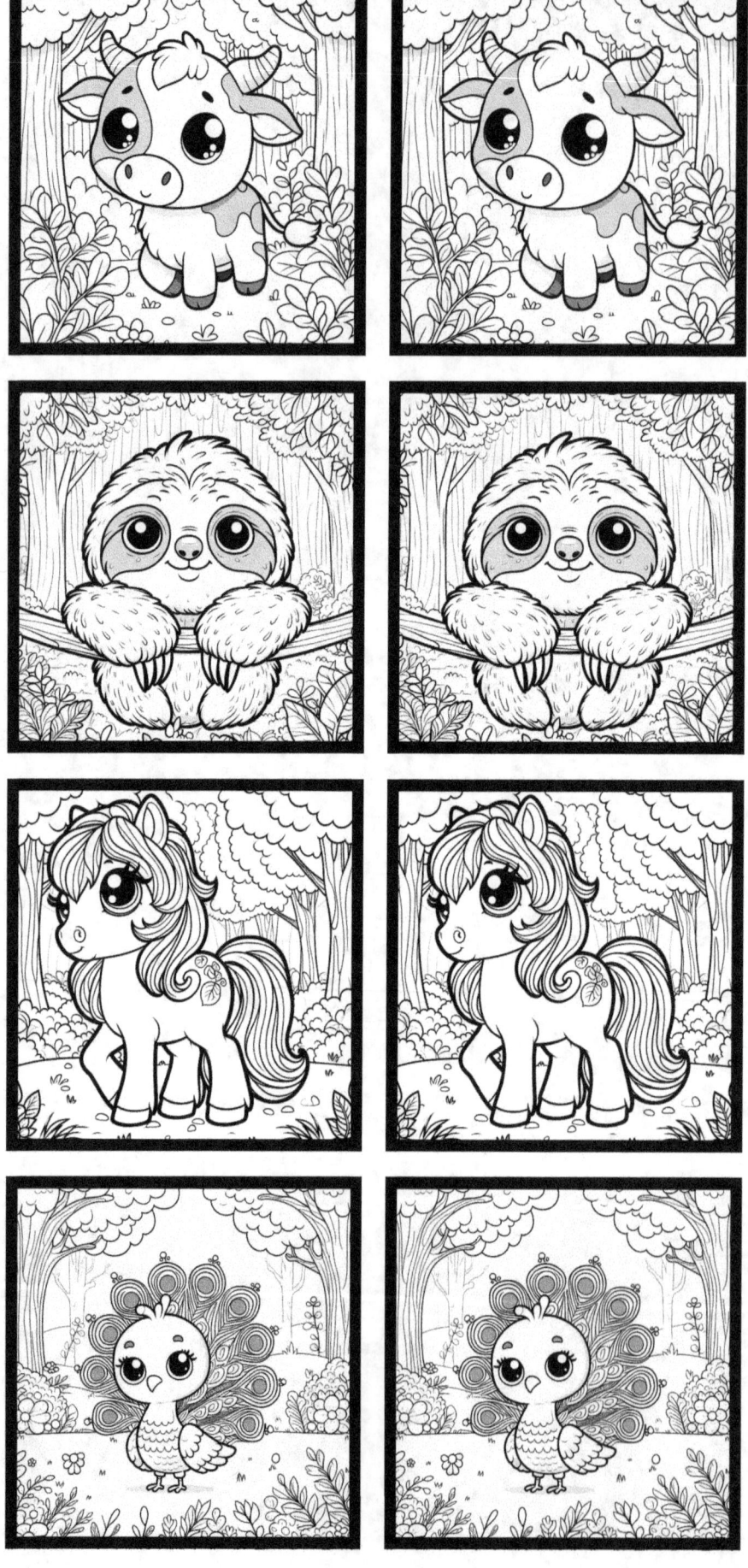

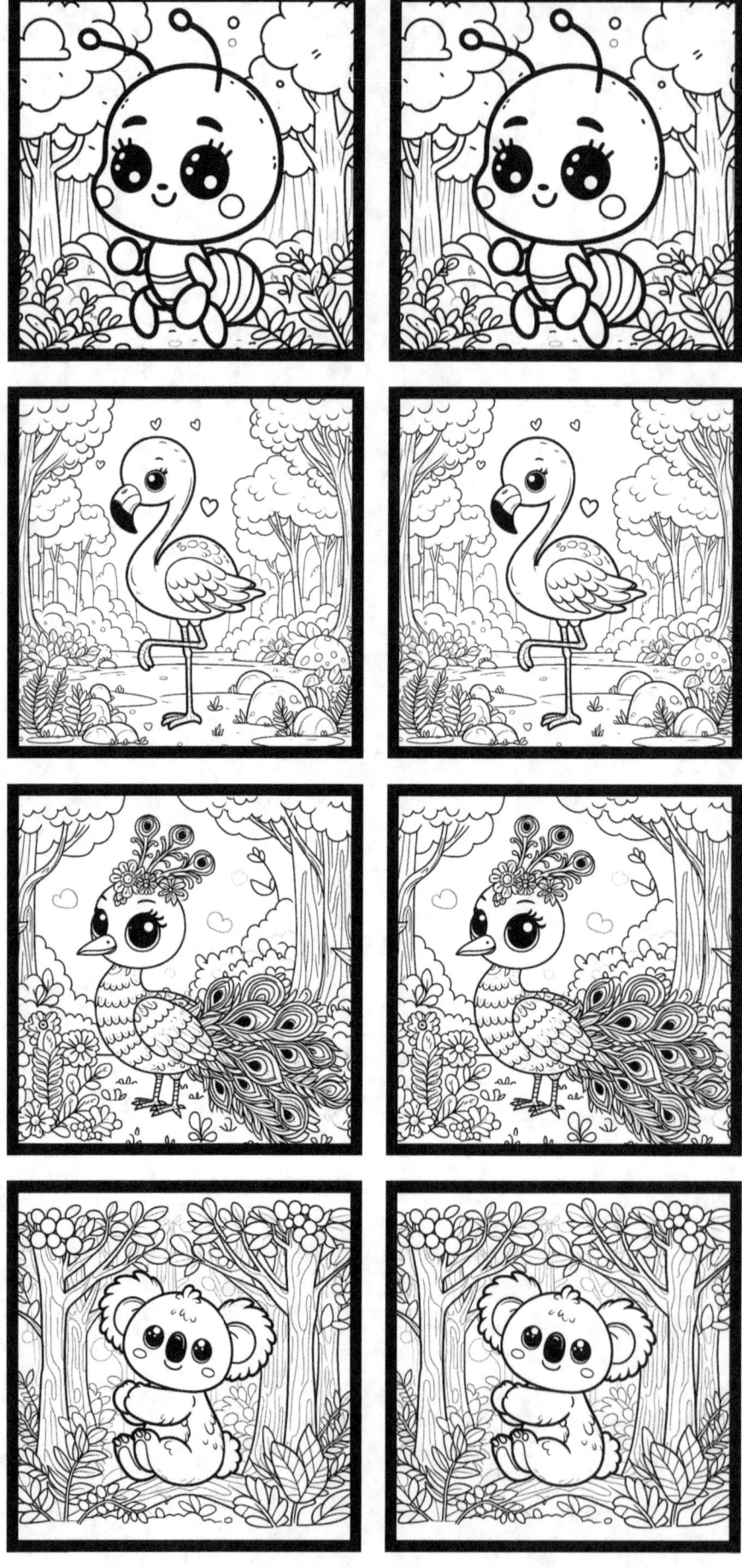

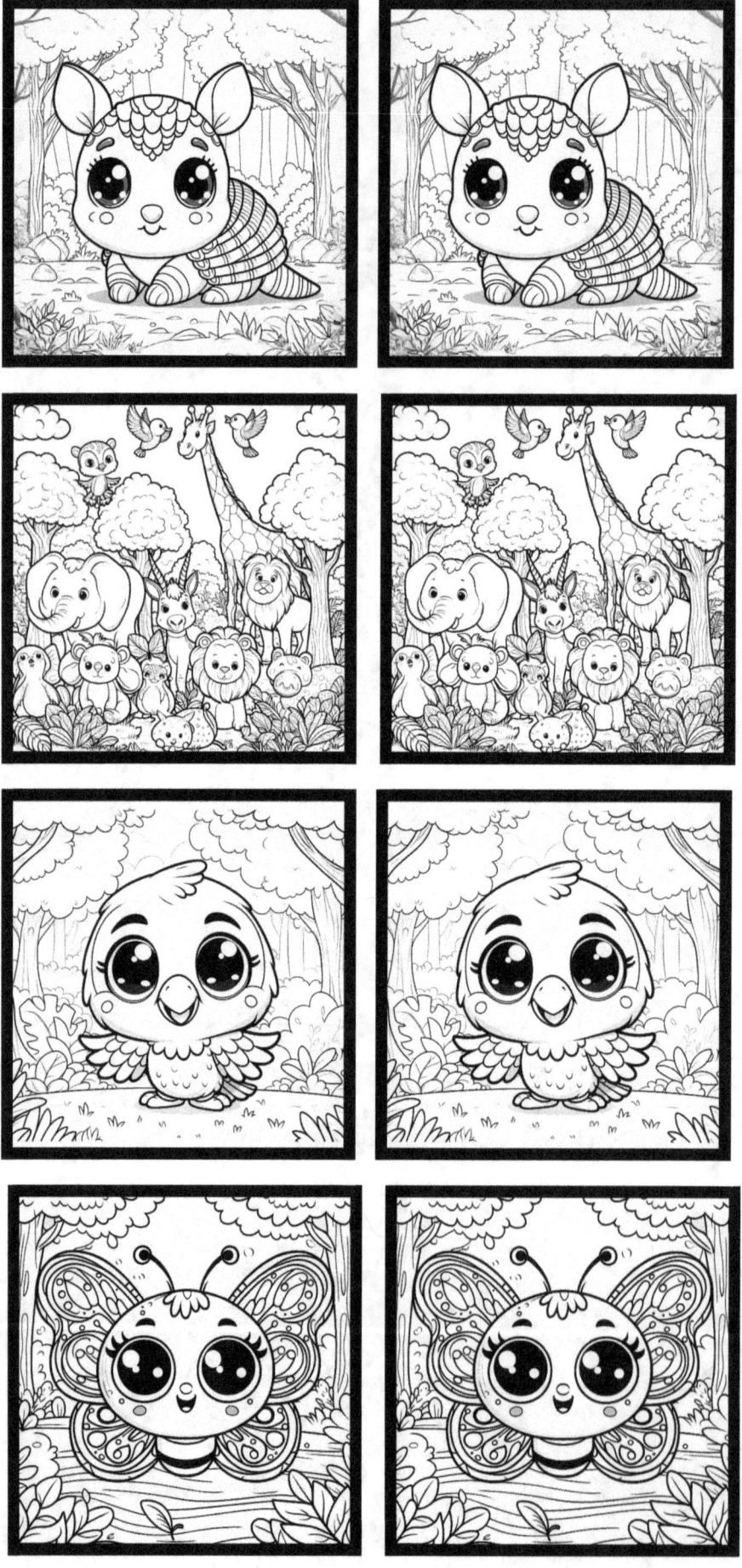

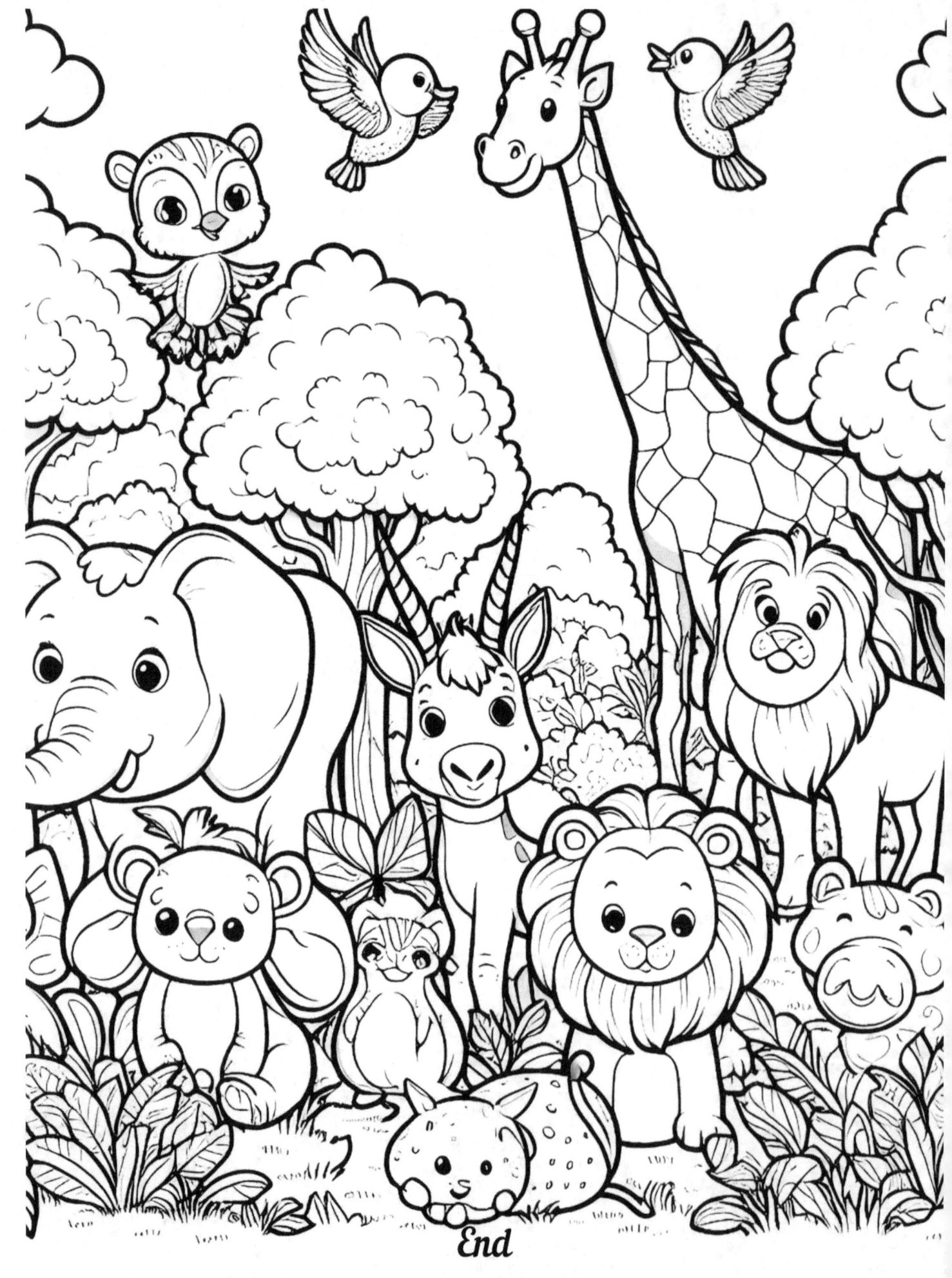